SOLVING FOR VALUE

SOLVING FOR VALUE

A Journey of Ambition and Stupidity

Enjoy the journey! :) Sander

Ryan Brook

By

Sander Dur and Ryan Brook

To Lucy, Oscar, Phoebe, and Poppy – you may not have known I was writing a book, but your love and support made it possible.

To Sander – we are never doing this again. – Ryan

To my amazing family. I would be nowhere without you.

To Ryan – Too late, I already started and put your name on it, too. – Sander

CONTENTS

Foreword by Dave West

As CEO of Scrum.org, I visit many organizations, speak frequently at conferences, and chat with many people about adopting Scrum, agility, and product delivery. These conversations tend to go something like this.

Person - "So, we have implemented Scrum, but are finding it has some challenges. What would you recommend?"

Dave – "Are the challenges about dependencies, work breakdown, planning, delivery, stakeholders, estimation, team composition, the role of management, metrics, human resources, hiring, skills..."

Person: "Yes."

Dave – "Well, nothing too challenging then :-)."

Change is hard, and bringing new ideas into complex, existing organizations is tough. The existing system does not want to change, and people don't want to change. And the customer still wants their new features when they want them.

So, how do you effectively adopt Scrum?

From experience, I have seen that the most effective method is to apply an incremental, outcome-oriented approach to adopting Scrum. You experiment with different strategies to achieve a clear goal that makes business sense, such as improving customer promoter scores, increasing customer engagement, or delivering more innovation into the market. This goal will guide your decisions about your agile practices and help you balance scale, dependencies, and focus. So, a straightforward, agile approach to adopting agile can be very effective—and it sounds simple enough!

However, the devil is in the detail. The nature of humans in big organizations is that there can be many false indicators. For example, if the business objective is to deliver more innovation to the market, it would seem natural to focus on velocity. How much "stuff" are the teams delivering? However, a focus on velocity can lead to delivering work with very little value and an almost religious focus on sizing and estimation. Which ultimately will reduce innovation and value. Add to that a lack of clarity about what good looks like, and you are back to square one, finding the adoption challenging and hard.

In *Solving for Value,* Sander and Ryan provide an approach that can support your agile adoption and have done so entertainingly and humorously. They describe the practices that often undermine your adoption, providing clear anchors to stabilize your approach. I particularly like how they focus on value, outcomes, and signals. These ultimately drive your adoption more than motion metrics such as velocity.

Throughout the book, they talk about the importance of self-management. Self-management is often overlooked as a key ingredient to agility at scale; instead, organizations focus on processes, tools, meetings, and dashboards. In fact, many organizations reduce self-management at scale by moving decision-making up the organization. Self-management is the reason why I love Scrum. The idea that we leverage the collective intelligence, energy and passion of everyone on a team to deliver amazing value is something that resonates with me. And I think this is based on my experiences working in large organizations. When I started my career journey in the early 90s, I was given work and a process to follow. The process and work often did not make sense, but I was told to get on with it. The reality is that the industrial approach to creative work is fundamentally flawed. Over time, I became less and less motivated and contributed less and less to the organization. Luckily, I escaped and started building amazing things again. Still, I look back at that time with a desire to help organizations leverage their people more effectively to develop organizations and processes where teams feel empowered to do valuable work and change things that do not make sense. Sander and Ryan have sprinkled this magic powder throughout their book. They describe how teams can own their destiny and give them a series of tools to help shape it. They promote ideas such as everyone interacting with the user and other stakeholders, the importance of transparency and accountability, and describe how leadership creates an environment where value is delivered and change is the norm.

The book is comprehensive and sometimes challenging, but the humor and style help the reader navigate. Its tone and style are unique and very different from those of other Scrum, agile, or management books. The jokes, cutouts, and commentary make the experience of reading this book very rewarding and educational. Throughout, the themes of value, outcomes, and fun provide a great north star.

Good luck with your agile adoptions. I hope this book provides support and a few agile jokes along the way.

Dave West CEO Scrum.org September 2024

Foreword by Maarten Dalmijn

I've stopped reading Scrum books. This may sound shocking, but please allow me to explain.

Most books about Scrum talk about the same things in the same boring way. Yes, I do know what the Scrum Guide says. No, you don't have to tell me again. I don't need yet another diagram explaining all the Scrum events and how they fit together. Yes, I know the difference between role and accountability since the change was made in 2020. There is no need for yet another rehash.

All this repetition makes reading Scrum books often feel like you're stuck in the movie Groundhog Day or a Star Trek time loop episode. It's extremely dull and exhausting. To make matters worse, most books are too theoretical, lacking stories to illustrate how it all works in the real world. There is little you can do but to stop reading, which is what I usually do.

I even started thinking, "Maybe I'm the problem." But then I began reading this book, and I couldn't stop. This book is *different*.

The word Scrum isn't even in the title, yet it talks about Scrum. It's fun and easy to read, yet sneaky in its depth. There is no endless theoretical rambling. Instead, two seasoned veterans get to the heart of the matter by enthusiastically sharing their stories and the scars they experienced while living in the trenches. *Solving for Value* effortlessly unwraps big ideas you can immediately apply to your daily work by talking about the Navy Seals, Dexter, and Sandra Bullock — leaving you smiling all the way through.

In short, study this book if you want a breath of fresh air. Read it if you want to laugh and if you want to be surprised about Scrum. And especially pay close attention if you want to learn how you can leverage Product Management practices to solve for value. *Solving for Value* brings the delivery of value to the forefront, with Scrum quietly humming in the background.

I'm delighted to leave you in Sander and Ryan's extremely capable hands to guide you on your journey beyond Copy-Paste Agile toward *Solving for Value.*

Maarten Dalmijn, author of *Driving Value with Sprint Goals,* 22 October 2024

INTRODUCTIONS

Why does this book exist?

Because we clearly have too much time on our hands, of course!

More seriously, despite our regular consulting jobs, teaching Scrum.org classes, speaking at conferences, hosting and guest-appearing on podcasts, writing articles, engaging with our Discord community, and our family life with kids, we noticed that there was a gap in the market for what we had to offer as two experienced Scrum practitioners. Even though Scrum is a human process, very little content is available that includes humorous anecdotes, client stupidity, and dry sarcasm—enter Ryan and Sander.

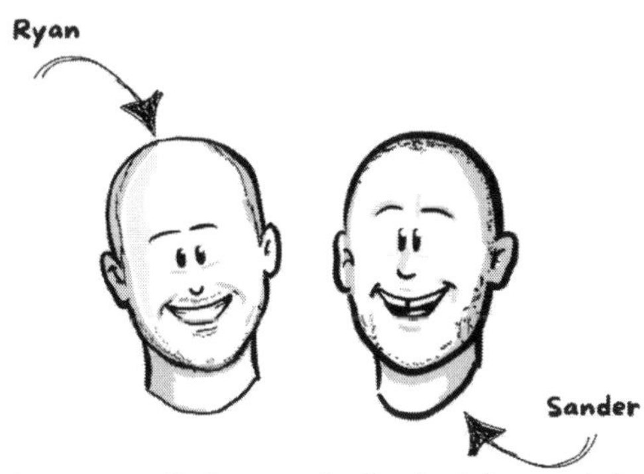

We want to offer lighthearted material that is also highly reflective and helpful to apply in practice. While many books out there paint a picture-perfect scenario of how product management *should* work, we specifically decided to surface some of the anti-patterns we, and the communities we engage with repeatedly face and offer insights and tips to effect change. To be clear, we want to combine humor with valuable insights.

As coaches, we enjoy provoking thought in others. As such, the reason we've written a book is an important one to us. Anyone who has done it before knows that writing a book takes a significant amount of time, and even if you haven't, you can probably guess (then multiply it by three—typical sizing practice, right?). Our primary driver for investing our time to write (and rewrite) this book is to produce a permanent and physical milestone that represents our mission to support the professional development of others. We're hopeful that it is a casual read, and we would love to hear your feedback if we decide to go through it again in the future. Before you commit to moving on to the next pages, let us share a joke with you.

One day, a Story Point and a developer were having a conversation.

"This work is going to be way easier than we first thought," said the developer.

"Phew! I wondered why I felt slightly inflated!" replied the Story Point.

(Author note: this is the quality level of jokes you can expect... you have been warned.)

Humor makes everything easier to deal with, and that's what we want to write about in this book. Importantly, we still want you to be able to look back after reading this book and say, "Hmm. Well, I've got some work to do to improve!" A Scrum Master's job is never done, and even though we know you already understand this, it never hurts to prove a point.

If you've heard of "rubber duck debugging," [1] consider this book as your rubber duck. Talk to it, argue with it, but most importantly, question it—that's how we believe you will get the most out of your effort in reading what is contained within these pages. There may be areas where you disagree with us, but that's okay. Scrum is a deeply human-centric framework, and as with most things in life, context is key, so don't be afraid to overlay your personal context with the scenarios and research we present.

Before we take you through the structure in more detail, we know we've implied it already, but please be advised that you are not about to read a professional book. There are far too many (bad) jokes and stories for it to be considered professional. But does that mean it's not valuable? As our good friend Ralph Jocham would say, "The only way you can determine value is by releasing it to the market." You are that market.

Something we see frequently with Scrum practitioners is a concluding, often self-validated argument that "our organization doesn't work like that." Beyond complex work, we know that there are alternative (and often better) frameworks for the job—you don't have to use Scrum! We decided to pick this particular

[1] *https://rubberduckdebugging.com/*

framework as we teach it and have been working in the trenches. It is the most dominant framework applied in organizations tackling complex problems. That's also where many antipatterns and dysfunctions have emerged. Lately, we've seen a shift in how organizations deal with product management. Let the lessons learned in this book guide you in your personal challenges, whatever framework, method, or process you apply. This is why whenever you read anything related to Scrum (and there's a lot) in this book, you can replace it with any other type of framework. The processes around changing and adapting to new ways of working are eerily similar in all new situations.

The learnings we share throughout this book are based on our experiences as consultants in the real world. We are, and continue to be, active practitioners working with organizations to improve their business agility. Many businesses would have you believe they are unique and the only ones ever to have a particular problem. Spoiler alert: they aren't (did we even need to write that bit?). This book helps you hold up a mirror to them and support the brilliant organizational change we know you are trying to help them achieve.

With respect to that change, we know that it is constantly made harder by achingly slow processes, cultures underpinned by lack of shared ownership, and sometimes just those "pain in the ass" people who you wish you could shake. Scrum describes itself as simple but never says it will be easy. Arguably, the boundaries imposed by many organizations that continuously make your life harder to effect change are the very reason they need you. If you've ever heard someone say that a client isn't willing to listen and that should move on; we can empathize with that viewpoint. However, please consider that struggling to listen vs. listening but choosing to ignore are different things. Psychologically, it's a tough position to be in, but potentially, it is where the most opportunities are to impart wisdom and develop the most value.

Whether it is the macro-organizational issues you face or the microcosm of single-team nuances (well, the team would call them nuances; you probably call them annoyances), please know that all Scrum practitioners worldwide are with you. The evidence of unprofessionalism is everywhere, so our call to action is to continue fighting the good fight. With that in mind, we recommend you move forward with your practice by initiating tough conversations with yourself, your teams, and your broader organization; only by gaining transparency can we meaningfully inspect and adapt.

Here are a few excerpts from two of Ryan's recent client conversations:

Ryan: *"I'd always recommend one Sprint Goal per Sprint so that the Developers can maintain focus."*

Client: *"No, no, more goals means we'll get more things in flight."*

Ryan: *"Do you want things started or finished?"*

Ryan: *"Here's a list of impediments we need organizational support to remove."*

Client: *"They sound like your problems need fixing, not mine."*

Ryan: *"But the first thing on the list is lack of organizational support..?"*

Structure

The book is written to address three themes; the practices that screw up your Scrum, how to anchor good practice, and finally, how you can leverage self-management to improve success. Each purpose has a different outcome, but fundamentally, they have been chosen to support your transition through Shu-Ha-Ri technique mastery.[2]

However, if you aren't willing to critically reflect on your practice and be called out, this probably isn't the book for you. If there were an unofficial Product Goal for this book, it would be:

"Arm our readers with the awareness and tools to metaphorically slap those who explain Product Management using Jira terminology."

(As an aside, this is not the last time we'll moan about Jira during this book. To all the Jira fanatics, consider yourself warned.)

So, how will we help you address these antipatterns and client "idiosyncrasies?" First, we're going to tell you a story. It's a story about a man named Roy and the company he works for: Magnum Opus. To be clear, Roy isn't like you. Roy is who you are happy not to be. If you see characteristics in Roy and think, *"That sounds like me,"* seek professional coaching immediately. But more on Roy later.

[2] *Alistair Cockburn, Humans and Technology Technical Report 2016.01 (2016)*

We'll take time to discuss the problem state, team kick-off, and how each Scrum Event can be leveraged to improve success.

Within each chapter that incorporates Roy and his team, there are three themes to look out for that may help you grasp what we're trying to achieve:

1. **Screwing Up Your Scrum** – We've all done things we aren't proud of, but how often do you reflect more generally on antipatterns that you or your broader organization tolerate or, worse still, intentionally implement? In many circumstances, silence and inaction can be considered acceptance. We're trying to re-invigorate your awareness of and intolerance to antipatterns. You will likely be experiencing some of them now, and we've always found it nice to know that the (Scrum) world isn't always perfect for other people either. Nothing is worse than someone saying, "Oh, really? You're having a problem? It seems to work fine for me."

   Allow us to point out poor practices, help you reflect on your current situation, and consider the impact of allowing those activities to continue. This represents mastering the "Shu" of the "Shu-Ha-Ri" technique.

2. **Anchoring Good Practice** – Once you're in a hole, it can be hard to climb back out. It's human nature to keep digging. We aim to provide concrete techniques and discussion to help you, the Scrum Team, and the organization get back on track. As Scrum Masters, everyone knows we love facilitation (it's our only job, right?). However, we'll include varied approaches and activities utilizing the different choices a Scrum Master can make to fulfill their accountability. Let us provide you with a toolkit to help. This represents "Ha."

3. **Self-Management Success** – Sometimes, being the sole Scrum fanboy/girl within a team can feel lonely. It's easy to become apathetic and fall into the aforementioned cycle when that happens. Like a good Product Backlog, you are also a living artifact, and your needs must be met. We'll share tips and tricks to do this, discussing mental health, conflict, and broader organizational coaching. We aren't aiming to guide you in your next steps but instead offer some ideas—the only person who knows what you need is you.

We hope this book will help you transcend thoughts of antipatterns and poor practices as existential and change your thought pattern to see opportunities for improvement. This represents "Ri."

How We'd Like You to Read This Book

As you settle in to read this book, grab a whiskey, beer, or any drink of your choice. If you're the kind of person who likes to annotate books (bearing in mind that they can never be re-sold on Amazon), then we'd like to think there will be a few things you'll find insightful enough to want to remember.

Over the years, we've found a few nice techniques to engage with books in a light-effort kind of way that you may find interesting:

- **Book on a Page**: Choose any size of card or paper you want (we recommend A6 because it will fit nicely within this book). As you progress, write down an occasional word or phrase you liked. The goal is not to summarize the book into a page but to minimize the 70,000-ish words into a single side of worthwhile notes. If you can keep this up for a few books a year, you are slowly building up succinct ideas that can probably be turned into your own book.

- **Colored Tabs**: Grab some tiny sticky tabs (limit yourself to 1 per chapter so the book doesn't look like a Christmas tree) and highlight individual pages. If you ever decide to re-open this book later, you can ignore things you didn't like and jump straight to the juicy stuff.

- **Tweet Along**: Create a personal (and private) Twitter account just for you. If you prefer a digital record of your notes, tweet the sentences you like. Remember to identify the book in each tweet so that you can follow it more effectively when you read your history back.

We'll try to help you with information summaries as much as possible by providing our own RSS feed at the end of every chapter. "Really Simple Syndication," we hear you ask? No, "Ryan and Sander's Summary," of course. We'll break down each chapter into the most apparent points we think are valuable enough to take away. Like most meetings that could have been email, this book could have just been a blog, but where would the fun be in that?

One final point before we dig in is that we don't want you to read this book looking for answers. As competent Scrum practitioners and product management professionals, the steps you must take can likely be found using reflective questions at the end of chapters for guided, personal coaching. Neither author knows your exact situation, and therefore, we'd encourage you to be empirical—try something and evaluate how it goes.

To share personal experiences and situations, we have created thought bubbles like this one, with the related author's cartoon next to it. These are meant to illustrate specific theories or share the stories from our work in the trenches.

Preflective Questions

Every practitioner considering or wanting to be a professional frequently engages in rigorous self-reflection and critique. Here is your first opportunity to do that. Please write your ideas down and answer the questions honestly. Unless you give this book away, no one else will read your answers, so there is no value in lying to yourself.

Describe your current team's strengths and weaknesses briefly.

What is your stake in those weaknesses? Do you accept equal ownership?

Pause and consider, what are you actively working on with your Scrum Team to improve (note, we're not asking you to come up with things now, just those things already in flight)?

How would your team/s describe your practice as a <insert your role here> (if you aren't sure, perhaps you should ask them)?

Were you honest? We hope you were.

1.

Founding for Value

"If you don't know where you're going, any road will get you there."

– Lewis Carroll

Preflective Questions

Scrum is easy to understand yet hard to implement. Its lightweight nature can cause misunderstandings and ambiguous executions of the framework. This book describes cases that contain many common misconceptions and wrongful executions of how Scrum is intended, followed by our experience and good practices to return to proper Scrum. Note that it says good practices, as empiricism has no best practices. The complexity requires situational leadership and decentralized decision-making. Every situation is different. Therefore, there is no "best."

When starting your work with your product team, there is always a certain degree of assumptions about the work ahead. The same goes for this book. Let's check in on what knowledge you currently possess about the origins of Scrum within your organization. At the end of the chapter, you will reflect on and identify any potential learnings. We have intentionally left space for you to jot down your thoughts. Remember, no one will read these responses other than you, so let the truth free you.

What was the original reason your organization implemented Scrum?

Were those who made that decision actively involved in the new Scrum Team(s)?

Magnum Opus

Meet Roy Mifflin. He lives with his wife and kids in the upper Pineappolis region. His career has steadily increased, facing little friction and minor challenges. Roy works as a project manager in the engineering department of a large organization called Magnum Opus. Magnum Opus develops security devices that are mostly used in government organizations. The products they built had been of good quality, supporting them in a leading market position. But in recent years, they started falling behind in some areas. Magnum Opus is trying to keep up with the competition, proving they can innovate faster and have salespeople that tell the client base exactly what they want to hear.

Last week, Roy had a tough conversation with CEO John Ira (J. Ira for short) and the CFO. Their competitors can deliver faster, which they noted as one of the biggest challenges. If the results keep going the way they are now, a round of layoffs will be needed to prevent bankruptcy later this year. Now, he has been equipped with the glorious task of coming up with a solution that will make his people deliver faster. He is left clueless about his next move.

To divert his thoughts, Roy turns to the birthplace of agile transformations: LinkedIn. Doomscrolling through a seemingly endless stream of posts about the best and fanciest methods and frameworks, he thinks Scrum would be a good fit to keep his fellow Opanites employed.

"After all, Scrum is about making teams perform quicker, right? Let's start this as soon as we possibly can."

Over the weekend, Roy dives into the Scrum Guide to figure out how this seemingly silver-bullet framework works and how he will implement that into

Engineering. "The engineers will probably not all be aligned on the mechanics of the framework and why we need to implement this straight away," he reasons, "but it's better than the alternative of not having a job at all."

Come early Monday morning, Roy presents his plan to the department. He gathers all 247 people in the auditorium to charm everyone with a motivational speech.

"Scrum is the perfect methodology that makes the teams deliver faster and save a ton of money. All we need is a Product Owner, who will be me, by the way, a Scrum Master to facilitate every meeting and keep the team happy, and the developers, being you! And the best thing about Scrum is that you can decide what to do all by yourself. Scrum Teams are autonomous; therefore, they decide what to do. For a Scrum Team to work, between three and nine people are needed. That means I still need seven developers and a Scrum Master."

"This is great! I definitely want to join that team. No one is ever going to bother me again if I can do whatever I want!" senior Java Engineer Peter nudges his colleague Johanna.

Being the more conservative and analytical of the two, Johanna has doubts but decides to try it as well. The pair of them, amongst about fifty others, emails Roy. Roy now has two rather challenging tasks:

- Getting the right people on board the Scrum Team
- Finding a Scrum Master, as no one wants to fulfill the role

To get the right people on the team, he appoints individuals based on his knowledge of who he deems get along well: one problem down, one to go. For the latter, he decides to hire an external person. To find this person, he resorts to the place where the idea for Scrum was born and Scrum Professionals seem find their gathering place. Part of the job description he lists is as follows:

As a junior Scrum Master, you will be part of a division within the Engineering department. You will make the customer-obsessed Scrum Team successful and ensure they deliver faster. As an autonomous team, you will pave the way to client satisfaction yourself and are empowered to do whatever it takes.

What you bring:

- Knowledge and experience with hardware manufacturing
- Experience as a project manager

- Proven track record as a facilitator
- Adept at managing project plans and resources to ensure successful project completion
- Strong Python experience
- Skills related to Risk Assessment and Management and how to control them
- Working with people with different functional expertise respectfully and cooperatively, ensuring full utilization
- Highly skilled in documentation
- Skilled in database reporting and use of relevant software like Crystal Reports, Access, or Excel

Must have: Expert in JIRA

Must have: Expert in MS Teams

Desired: PSM III

After having multiple interviews with potential candidates, accompanied by HR, a decision is made to hire Jax Franklin as the new Scrum Master. Now the team is complete. Together, they can start saving the company from a seemingly certain downfall.

Meet the team:

Roy - Product Owner
Jax - Scrum Master
Johanna - Senior Software Engineer
Peter - Senior Software Engineer
Ronda - Junior Designer
Madhuri - Software Engineer
Laurens - Database Engineer
Mackenzie - Java Virtual Machine Engineer
Alexii - Test Engineer

<u>*Where do we go from here?*</u>

Fortunately, this case example combines many things going wrong simultaneously. Rarely does this happen as described. Nonetheless, the portrayed situations do happen frequently. It begins by understanding the problems you are trying to solve and identifying options to find a solution. Scrum might be one of those solutions, but we want to clarify that this framework is by no means a silver bullet that magically helps remove all issues in the organization. If anything, it will start to make *existing*, potentially latent issues transparent. Then, you have one of two choices:

- Face the issues head-on and appropriately deal with them;
- Ignore the issues and point fingers at people or things.

We chose the first option to ensure we have enough content to continue writing this book. Let's go back to the drawing board to understand MO's issues.

Taking Accountability

In the previous paragraph, the organization's continued existence is being placed on the shoulders of a single team. This might not always be the case, yet individual teams have the power to make or break the achievement of common goals.

From this point on, the definition of success is the achievement of goals. These could be any type of goal: Product Goals, Sprint Goals, Organizational goals, or even personal goals. Success does not equate to high revenue unless specified as such.

Through our experience, we've discovered that organizations often fail to understand what they are trying to achieve. Frequently heard reasons for the implementation of Scrum are:

- We need to deliver faster;
- We want to save money;
- The competition is doing it too;
- To do twice the amount of work;
- *"Err, it seemed like a good idea because of all those people on LinkedIn."* We kid you not; we have heard this more often than we would like to admit.

There are all kinds of reasons for perceived improvement. After asking questions about the current state of business, like the delivery rate, people more often stay quiet rather than being presented with a baseline against which to measure improvements.

That leads us back to the question of what problem we're trying to solve. After all, it's hard to create a solution without demand for it. In this example, competition can do things that Magnum Opus itself can't do in its current state. These factors cannot be ignored, even if you have a competitive edge. Ignoring variables around you could lead to what have now become classic case studies like Nokia,[3] Blockbuster,[4] or Kodak.[5] Spoiler alert: they didn't adapt to changing circumstances, underestimated threats, and are now either a glimpse of what they used to be or wholly ceased to exist.

That's where the challenge is hidden. Creating transparency, or a burning platform, is necessary for people to understand why change is needed. On the flip side, what would happen if they didn't change? If there is no understanding of *why,* things will stay as they are. As Simon Sinek puts it, *Start with Why.*[6]

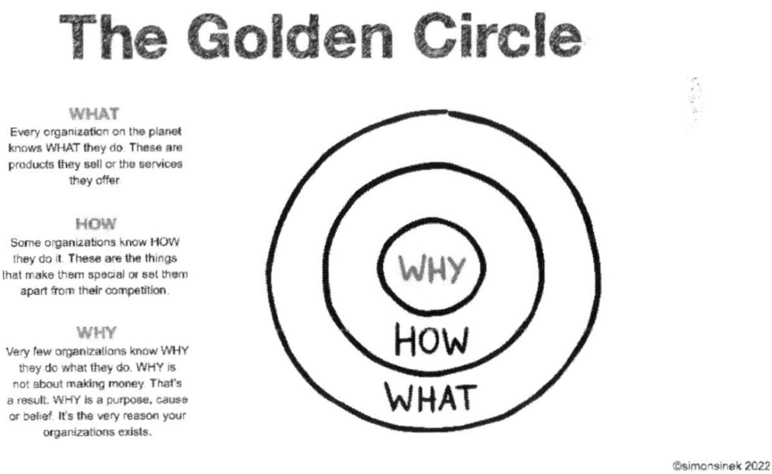

Figure 1 - Golden Circle - simonsinek.com/golden-circle/

[3] *Tuomo Peltonen, Towards Wise Management (Helsinki: Springer International AG), 168*

[4] *https://www.mbaknol.com/management-case-studies/case-study-how-netflix-took-down-blockbuster/*

[5] *https://www.forbes.com/sites/chunkamui/2012/01/18/how-kodak-failed/*

[6] *Simon Sinek, "Start with Why: How Great Leader Inspire Everyone to Take Action"(Portfolio, 2011)*

Understanding why we change and its impact makes people want to do better. Think about small children. If you ask kids to do something, they'll often ask, "Why?" If they understand why it is what you want them to do, a mental assessment is made about consequences, pros and cons, followed by actions. They see the reasoning behind it, whether they agree with it or not. We want to challenge you to be that kid in the organization who *wants* to understand. Ask why until you do.

The case of Magnum Opus is a classic example of how the entire organization needs to change accordingly. There is an apparent reason for change. Suppose they apply the ostrich strategy (sticking their heads in the sand, pretending not to see any problems). In that case, competitors will swiftly and relentlessly take over, and MO will be out of business. That is where we often see strategy starting to split ways with vision. Roy has chosen Scrum for the sake of faster delivery. Faster delivery doesn't mean guaranteed survival. Even though he understands the consequences of not changing, his message of "faster delivery" (or any other unintended yet expected benefit of Scrum) sets false expectations—semantics matter.

Scrum is a framework for delivering value and limiting risk. Anything else can have an assorted effect, but it is not the purpose of Scrum.[7]

Define the Product

When you know what challenges you must overcome, a deep dive can be made on the way forward. Many factors contribute to the overall success of a company:

- Products & Strategy;
- Culture;
- Ability to change;
- Market spread;
- Understanding market needs;
- Available resources (no, people are not resources).

This book will cover every topic to a shorter or longer extent. Magnum Opus understands its burning platform, which it now needs to get off of: if they don't adapt to changing circumstances, it negatively impacts its daily operations.

[7] *https://www.scrum.org/resources/what-is-scrum*

Roy thought of a highly sensitive iris scanner allowing users to access certain parts of their building that they only need access to. Employees would be scanned while approaching an area so they wouldn't have to swipe a card or any other badges. He envisioned a seamless experience in the future.

"Access in the blink of an eye."

None of MO's competitors offers such a product. This could be the break they need to get a competitive edge. This Product Vision Statement doesn't mention how the product will look and operate. It's too early to say anything about the details at this stage. The future is uncertain, and the team doesn't know yet how they will exactly build it. Any extensive detailing at this point is futile, as the time invested in detailing will need to be redone by the time they start building the specific features and components.

This product brings a lot of uncertainty to the organization. It's a new product, it hasn't been tried before, and it's innovative. Roy and his team are uncertain how it will be created. There's little clarity about the exact requirements and technology. This is precisely the hook MO needs to figure out how they could try to build the product.

Product Definition

Implementing any framework has specific implications for how business is conducted. Proper understanding is required, more than simply reading a book or guide. Whatever you do, never treat any framework, methodology, or mindset as the solution. Solutions come in the form of products with certain aspects to satisfy customer needs. Customers don't need you to execute a framework properly; they have zero interest in that.

Picture a potential customer walking into a car dealer. She's been driving her old car for twenty years, and it's at the end of its lifecycle. She sees all the latest models, one after another, safer, more fuel efficient, and higher quality (top three most important factors[8] when buying a new car). She is about to place her order. What a great feeling! Suddenly, the salesman starts his informative story and tells her exactly how the car is being built and what molds the production plant uses. As a customer, she doesn't care how her new car is constructed. She only cares

[8] *https://www.statista.com/chart/13075/most-important-factors-when-buying-a-car/*

that the car gets her from A to B safely, with high fuel efficiency and high-quality materials. That's all about the product and meeting her needs.

The same goes for implementing Scrum. Scrum isn't a magic wand that people can point at their organizational issues and **poof**, the problems are gone. It merely provides a foundation that, if appropriately applied, forms a means to an end. Not the end itself. Implementing Scrum without understanding the impact and potential changes in the organization is the equivalent of building your house on quicksand. It seems to work fine initially, but soon, you will see the expected benefits drowning due to poor decision-making. This may sound like an open door, but our experience teaches us that short-term thinking and starting without understanding how Scrum works is more common than you might think.

This is what makes a framework different from a methodology. Frameworks are like the walls of a house. They provide you with the boundaries, but you still decide how you are most comfortable living between those walls.

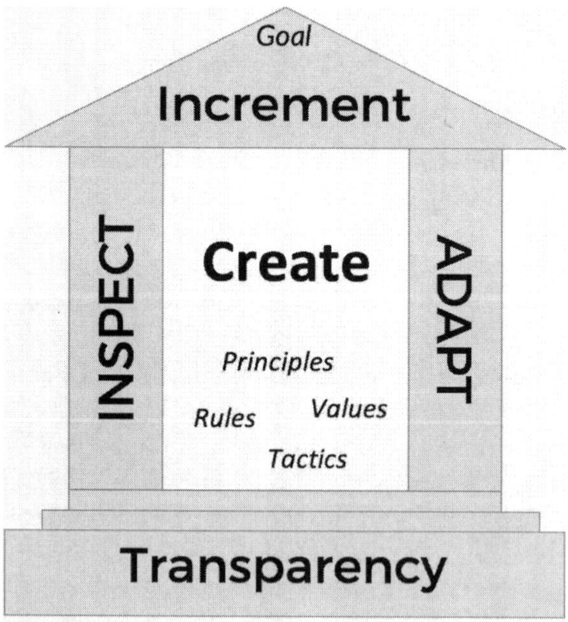

Figure 2 - The House of Scrum by Gunther Verheyen

"The House of Scrum is an inclusive house of warm, open, and collaborative relationships, not a house that ***excludes*** *people." – Gunther Verheyen*

By only providing boundaries, self-management, and autonomy are supported. A methodology would do the exact opposite: it would be prescriptive in telling you how to live within your home. Although methods have their place in the workspace, the complexity and (unknown) factors where Scrum operates turn off their practical use. Prescriptive steps of how to operate minimize the opportunity to respond to change, capitalize on new opportunities, or limit risk. Another undesired side effect of methodologies in complex domains is that they allow people to stop thinking about the best option given the circumstances. Only the methodology is being executed, leading to suboptimal results.

Understanding what domain of agreement and certainty your environment operates in can provide valuable input when choosing the right option for your organization. The Stacey Matrix[9] was created to understand these factors. In short, there are five main areas:

- **Simple domain (Princell, Waterfall)**: close to certainty, close to agreement;
- **Complicated domain (KanBan, Lean)**: close to certainty, far from agreement;
- **Complicated domain (KanBan, Lean)**: close to agreement, far from certainty;
- **Complex domain (Scrum)**: low in agreement, low in certainty.
- **Chaos domain (Lean Startup)**: far from certainty, far from agreement.

Scrum resides in that complex domain, and that's where empiricism comes in. People who are performing the work know how to do it best. Alternatively, we recommend checking out the Cynefin framework by Dave Snowden. Decentralized decision-making is at the heart of the Scrum Team. No one tells them how to perform the work to get the best result. That might require investment in time to reach a certain knowledge level, but it supports the general development of knowledge workers. Given time, they will learn more than executing how someone else in the organization tells them how to do it. This also means that not everything can be done with Scrum. Following a barbecue recipe, building an urban area, or doing operation-like activities in organizations are some areas that could be a better fit with different approaches. To each its own.

[9] *Stacey RD. Strategic management and organisational dynamics: the challenge of complexity. 3rd ed. Harlow: Prentice Hall, 2002.*

Rethinking organizational structure is highly recommended to make Scrum work. One common argument is, "Scrum will never work here." The main reason is trying to map Scrum to the existing organization instead of being courageous and thinking about what to change to make it work.

When we consider that Scrum is there to develop and deliver value in complex product environments, it's often easy for us to get wrapped up in the 'how we deliver" conversation. However, often, the more significant issue isn't the correct application of a framework but rather the definition of the problem space you're trying to address. Fundamentally, it comes down to what your "product" actually is. If you had to stand up tomorrow and clearly explain it to another team, could you do it?

With the distinct lack of experienced and knowledgeable Product Owners and Product Managers in organizations, it perhaps shouldn't be a surprise that product definition is poorly defined. In many organizations, the product they refer to singularly is a collection of products, and this frequently manifests in development situations like:

- *We can't craft a single Sprint Goal because we're working on too many things simultaneously.*
- *We can't get to Done because there's too much to integrate.*
- *We can't keep our Product Backlog under control because it actually has three products within it... AAAAAH!*

These issues are common and often considered the fault of the teams doing the work. But in reality, it's quite understandable that they struggle to self-manage successful delivery when their product boundaries are unknown or, at best, poorly defined—to quote Gino D'Acampo, "If my grandmother had wheels, she would have been a bike."

To share a bit of truth we've uncovered over many years of consulting, part of this poor product definition is down to the culture of acceptance. Budgets are being cut, fewer teams are available, and there's an appetite for innovations to be worked on, all culminating in a single team working on multiple threads at a time. This happens because your teams are too scared to push back and tell you, "NO!" Those organizations that truly support a product-centric environment need to be called out here—by splitting a team's focus multiple times, you aren't getting more work. You're getting less, and almost certainly at a lower quality. Giving a team a new product to work on while expecting them to maintain the delivery of a previous one is nothing less than a lack of respect, and we're here to tell you that your teams are noticing. They realize when they're overworked. They know when you're doing things detrimental to their value delivery. It breeds an attitude of carelessness about the products under their care because, quite frankly, they don't have the time to pour their love into it. After all, you've maxed them out. When product development becomes transactional, the human benefits of agility are being eroded.

If you want to help your organization move forward from this situation, you (and they) probably won't like the answer. We'll give you a short activity to try with them now, and it will hopefully end in a "holy sh*t" moment on their part.

Get your immediate senior leadership in a room co-located synchronously.

Lay out a list of all the products worked on in your department and get them to rank their importance to the users from greatest value to least value. Every single client should know their most valuable products, and if they don't, well, they've got some work to do. Follow this by laying out a list of the teams in your department and who is currently working on which product. This will likely be a one-to-many relationship.

If the penny drops, allow the silence. If it doesn't, ask them what their observations are about each team's loading level compared to the ordering of their most valuable products. Your goal is to get them to understand that they can't have everything. As painful as that will be for them to learn, they just can't. When you ask a child what their favorite toy is, they will initially be unable to decide, perhaps picking up two or three. If you challenge them, they should be able to put them in an order of value to them, knowing that in a fire, they could only carry so many. To tie this into organizations, the sheer delusion of some can be shocking to the point of disbelief at their inability to know what is valuable. "Everything!" they say. That answer often shows their real weakness—that they don't know.

Here are some reflective questions that you could use to help your clients understand that team capacity isn't unending:

- If the team stopped working on Product X, who would be impacted and why?
- If our organization was suddenly cut in half, what would we throw our effort behind?

- Would you rather three products progress slowly or one product get finished?

To directly provide the answer we alluded to earlier, the trick to getting yourself out of the never-ending rut of too many products and too few teams is to stop. You must make impactful and tough decisions about which toys (products) to put down. The newest toy may be the coolest thing to play with, but you can only play with (develop) a certain number at a time.

If your clients are unwilling to make tough decisions, then we hope you share with them this anecdote:

Figure 3 - Roy has his smart moments. Sometimes.

The takeaway is that knowing your product definition is key to successfully maintaining focus. Without a clear boundary, it's too easy to absorb more work and less easy to say no. After all, anything can be absorbed into an undefined blob and balloon your Product Backlog before you can say, "How did our Jira Backlog become 3,000 items long?" Another way we like to refer to these Product Backlogs is Marshmallow Backlogs. They look big and they're fluffy without too much content.

> *I once worked with a Scrum Team whose Product Backlog contained just over 2,000 Product Backlog Items that seemingly were still important. To cut a long story short, we made a forecast by extrapolating our current velocity to see how long it would take to complete, assuming we added nothing else to it. How long would it have taken, you may ask? Somewhere between 4-6 years.*

Overloading a single product to the point where it becomes multiple products that are inextricable from one another is a downward spiral. The only way out is to stop: cut products, and clearly define the problem each one is trying to solve. If you can't, you aren't building a product; you're building a monster.

Guide Until Needed

Once the decision has been made to continue with Scrum, our experience is that teams are expected to be autonomous overnight. Unfortunately, reality hits differently. Think of it as learning to ride a bicycle. Expecting this overnight change is the equivalent of giving your three-year-old a bike and saying, "See you at Grandma's. Good luck!"

> *My personal parenting experience has taught me that letting go without proper guidance causes serious damage to the desire to learn afterward. Or to quote my son: "NO, I DON'T WANT TO RIDE THIS STUPID BIKE ANYMORE!"*

People who aren't used to being in control of decision-making can find it daunting or even become anxious when, from one moment to the next, they're expected to make choices that can have significant effects. Equally, people can have different expectations of what self-management and autonomy mean. More on that in *"Boundaries."*

Scrum introduces three accountabilities: knowing the developers, the Product Owner, and the Scrum Master. As you will discover throughout this book, these accountabilities often differ from how business has been done before.

Factors like these that might require change (amongst others):

- Leadership;

- Shared goals;
- Boundaries;
- Clear accountabilities. [10]

This is by no means an exhaustive list. More factors need to be taken into account and tailored to your local context. We never want to hear (or read on LinkedIn), "Ryan and Sander said to discuss these four factors," while there might be twenty factors in your organizations that play a part in establishing self-management.

Leadership

Leaders are supposed to lead. In any transformation or adoption of new frameworks, they lead and are an example for others. Note that leaders are not the same as managers by default. Managers are an example of leaders, but Scrum Masters, Product Owners, and Developers can be leaders just as well. In the ideal world, these people are clearing the path for others to follow. This implies that the leaders have obtained sufficient in-depth knowledge to identify areas where to start and what to change. The term "leader" is often confused with (higher) management, whereas our experience tells us the roles are frequently trained later stage, if trained at all. The problem is that they're looked upon as leaders, while in reality, they don't lead anything. Those are not leaders; those are laggers.

Implementing Scrum when transitioning from a traditional, more conservative approach to development is a paradigm shift in mindset. We highly recommend not to underestimate the effect this has on behavior and the time it takes to fully get an agile mindset ingrained into your organization's culture. Imagine yourself having your driver's license for years, and you drive your car daily. You are accustomed to the response of your steering wheel. When you turn your steering wheel to the left, the vehicle will follow the same direction. Logical consequence. You've been doing it like this forever. Now that paradigm shift in mindset comes in, and from now on, you'll go to the right when you turn the wheel left. Such a change is not something you get used to overnight, but it will take time to become the new standard. Adopting an agile mindset and the use of proper Scrum is no different. Executing the framework itself is easy. Plan the events, and you're done. However, reaping the benefits as intended is a different story. It vastly differs from traditional meetings and, therefore, requires an approach tailored to local circumstances.

[10] *Ockerman & Reindl, Mastering Professional Scrum (Pearson Education Global), 32*

Running through the events without using them as intended is called mechanical Scrum or Zombie Scrum.[11] Scrum Teams seemingly are doing the right thing, but in reality, they barely scratch the surface of the possible. Persevering and situational leadership are required to keep the implementation heading in the right direction.

Leaders are great. It stands to reason, obviously, that we need them to be successful in product delivery, but what follows that simple statement is a thought about where those great leaders come from. Are they cultivated like plants in a garden? Do they pop up randomly like weeds? Or are they borne from the combined circumstances of environment and desire? Let's discuss the current models of leadership in many organizations and our observations on them.

To elaborate on this idea, consider the hierarchy in which you currently exist and whether it offers you any value. What do you get from your immediate "superiors?" You see, history has led us to believe that top-down management and, by extension, having control is most successful when those with the most experience centralize decision-making.

The problem with that is that it's wrong. It's a Tayloristic view that may have worked for complicated, factory-line work but fundamentally doesn't fit with complex product development. The principle behind empirical delivery is that those closest to the problem address the problem. Luckily, there's a simple solution to tackle this malformed idea of centralized decision-making, and that is to have more leaders. Hear me out, though, because we're not referring to leaders in the form you are (likely) imagining.

You might be familiar with the leader-follower archetype. A leader leads, and a follower follows. A follower may be knowledgeable, but their decision-making is deferred to the leader. This relationship is comfortable for many people but has been proven less effective than the competing archetype; leader-leader. The idea is that great leaders create great leaders. It's not about hierarchy and structure but about self-management and autonomy. Allow us to share two example conversations to illustrate this:

Leader-Follower

Follower: *"I've been looking into it, and I think it would be good to make this change to the product. What do you think?"*

[11] *Schartau, Verwijs & Overeem, the Zombie Scrum Survival Guide (Pearson Education Global)*

Leader: *"I would approach it by doing X, then Y, then Z."*

Follower: *"Okay, I'll do that."*

Leader-Leader

Leader 1: *"I've been looking into it, and I'm planning to make this change to the product."*

Leader 2: *"You're closer to the problem than me. If you think it's the right thing to do, just do it."*

Looking at both of these conversations, the problem doesn't change, but the solution becomes further removed from the one who knows the most about it, which sounds counter-intuitive. And it is. The follower seeks validation and accepts solutions provided by someone else. Whatever reason they do so, possibly:

- To reduce ownership in case something goes wrong;
- To follow organizational sign-off culture;
- To lessen their individual cognitive load.

But in all cases, you lose something in a leader-follower relationship, irrespective of the resultant solution. You lose the follower's ability to own their work (the problems and successes). This cycle is also self-reinforcing, whereby the autonomy of the person doing the work diminishes to the point of leader-servant.

Cultivating a leader-leader environment is remarkably simple. One additional thing to bear in mind is that Taylorism is over one hundred years old. Its applicability in modern complexity is questionable at best. Always keep an open mind to different approaches. More on leadership in Chapter 10.

I once worked in a team where I held a senior leadership position. It felt risky to start with, but whenever I was approached to make a decision, my response was always, "Well, what do you think we should do? Do that." Empowerment is not about passing accountability to someone else but about delocalising it away from a single point.

Shared Goals

Shared goals give everyone involved something to focus on and to measure progress toward. When these goals are clear and understood by everyone, the probability of delivering valuable products that meet or exceed the stakeholders' expectations increases. These goals must be made transparent. How that needs to be done is up to the Scrum Team to decide.

The only goals at Roy's current stage are to prevent bankruptcy and create a sensitive iris scanner for government building access restrictions. As more is uncovered and development progresses, more detailed goals will arise.

Boundaries

As mentioned, the framework is like a house. A house provides the structure within which you can operate. Walls are its boundaries, or in the case of Scrum, fourteen elements provide the outer bounds. Time boxes are in place to create a sense of urgency, provide focus, and reduce waste. This book will discuss every event specifically, and we challenge you to consider whether you and your team are using the events as intended.

Another great example, and one of those fourteen elements, is the "Definition of Done." It provides the team with minimal quality requirements and ensures that this specific boundary is met as a minimum before the Increment goes into production.

Boundaries of decision-making and what kind of support is required are not sucked out of thin air. Alignment is needed. Maybe your Scrum Team isn't yet at a level where you and/or the organization want them to be. Discuss its current and desired state and what can be done to progress slowly toward the desired state. This could mean the team needs specific subject matter experts (SMEs) to bring in during refinement or planning events or to inform others about their decisions.

Clear Accountabilities

Scrum has clear accountabilities in the form of the Scrum Master, Product Owner, and Developers. Choosing the Scrum framework implies that people are given specific authority to act according to their accountabilities and that the organization respects them. This can cause friction when these are not aligned during the changing phases. The activities and levels of decision-making Scrum brings are different from most traditional approaches and require transparency to thrive.

As with all change, time is required for new elements and behaviors to stick. Courage is needed to make inefficiencies transparent, whether they are behaviors or processes. Sometimes, people might feel anxious or insecure about change. The only way to deal with that is to make that, too, transparent.

One of the most frequent questions when teaching our Professional Scrum courses is whether one could fulfill multiple accountabilities, such as being a Product Owner and Scrum Master simultaneously. Or a Developer and Scrum Master. Technically, nothing is stopping you from doing so. Whether it's a great idea is a different thing. Are you able to keep an objective perspective from each individual accountability? When do you respond according to which one? What if both accountabilities are needed at the same time in different places? Again, you could, but should you? Are you able to truly fulfill the respective accountabilities if you're wearing multiple hats?

Alone We Can do so Little, Together We Can do so Much

Yes, we're quoting Helen Keller here. She was absolutely right, though. It's called team development for a reason, not individual within a group of others entirely unrelated to development. In the case of Magnum Opus, we saw that only Jax knows about the Scrum framework, while Roy read the Scrum Guide once, and the rest of the team doesn't know anything about Scrum. If they want this development effort to succeed and ensure the company's future existence, they all need to understand this paradigm shift in ways of working. Imagine the Navy SEALs suddenly deployed as a high-level basketball team. Something *completely* different. Only the team captain understands the rules and mechanics of the game; the rest just tag along without having a clue what to do and why. If the understanding of the rules is shared and they experience development together, they can rapidly grow as a team regardless of their backgrounds.

We don't want to sound like Apple, which advises you to use Apple; however, attending a course together as a team supports anchoring the new ways of working simultaneously. You get the opportunity as a team to ask your questions, and you all move in the same direction. Magnum Opus is lucky enough to have Jax on board with a proper understanding of Scrum. If Roy alone had led this change, it could have gone sideways quite fast. Many of the misconceptions and understandings in this book could have been avoided by just attending a course together. We understand and appreciate that this can be quite an investment in the short term. In the long term, the damage that is being done by not understanding or plain wrongful execution can render your team with many missed opportunities to inspect and adapt or to capitalize on new opportunities and lower risk.

"But we can do self-study too, right? Why should we spend that much money?"

What a great question! We're glad you brought that up. Professional trainers make a living by instilling this knowledge and building upon experience from the trenches. Most organizations that employ professional trainers, like Scrum.org, require you to bring at least four years of experience in the field. Supplementing the course with practical examples and the opportunity to ask questions or clarify certain topics is invaluable. The Scrum Guide is a picture-perfect Scrum world. While we would love nothing more than to see organizations apply the rule first, the practical world doesn't work this way. Granted, the exams can be passed by conducting self-study. Like cohort-based classes, self-study doesn't provide an applied understanding of the content.

We both are professional trainers and teaching classes on a weekly basis. We are also consultants. This works both ways in our humble opinion; you can't be a proper trainer without having experienced your own content and how challenging it can be. Equally, we think you can't be an effective consultant without a solid theoretical foundation to understand the rules of the game.

We would even go as far as to say it would be a great idea to involve the leaders in the organization to tag along with your team. People in power often make decisions about matters they don't understand. Magnum Opus has managers involved who are empowered to make decisions about Roy's team, but they don't understand the way the team works or how the product comes to fruition. Cracks in dynamics emerge, and people are more reluctant to speak up, as they might feel "it doesn't matter what I think anyway."

Ultimately, Scrum Teams are like plants. One can expect a plant to grow independently, but not much will happen. A more likely scenario is that it will look like Sander's living room. Plants are perishing because they are being neglected. Only with suitable soil, pH value, nutrition, lighting, temperature, and potentially more factors than Sander's minimal botanical knowledge allows him to jot down will plants grow.

Figure 4 - Allow organizational gardeners to create the environment.

Scrum Teams are no different. Without the right environment, they won't grow and can't deliver their full potential. As mentioned earlier, these elements need to be clear and aligned together with a psychologically safe environment and proper guidance so the people performing the work can flourish. Too often, Scrum Teams are expected to manage on their own and are being held accountable for not maximizing the benefits Scrum can bring. Organizations shoot themselves in the foot yet look around to see where the shot came from.

Ryan and Sander's Summary Feed (RSS Feed)

If there are any points that we want you to take away from this chapter, they are as follows:

- A thorough understanding of the challenges that need to be overcome is core to finding the right solution (is Scrum really the right way for our organization?).
- Don't start using Scrum without thoroughly understanding how to apply it and what changes might be necessary—organizational structure, people and their titles, desired culture, or product structure.
- Define what self-management and value mean in the context of your organization.
- Leaders should pave the way for others to follow.
- Proper training is essential in understanding the ways of working.
- Training only a lucky bunch and expecting them to change the entire organization is Utopia and has the potential to inflict more harm than it does good.

Reflection

Use this page to reflect on the initial questions at the beginning of this chapter and what you may have uncovered throughout.

What do you personally need to be more effective?

What can you do to support the understanding and impact of the change in ways of working?

How is fear of change being dealt with, and how does this relate to a sense of consistency?

2.

Starting the Journey Toward Value

"The single word that matters most, I think, to keep the company productive as it grows is alignment."

–Sam Altman

Preflective Questions

Every implementation has to start somewhere. The previous chapter concluded after forming the team. There is a distinction between a group of individuals working together. But by just putting highly skilled people together, it doesn't make it a team yet. Putting Ronaldo, Messi, Benzema, and Salah together would probably be a terrible choice, even though they are considered the best football (yes, football. Actual football, not the one predominantly played with hands) players in the world. It takes more than that. Before returning to Magnum Opus, we would like you to consider a few things.

What is the difference, to you, between a group of people working simultaneously and a team?

What does it take to be a great team?

What kind of behavior is detrimental to a team?

One month later, the first Sprint is a week away from starting. Due to the change in ways of working, the project manager who would usually work on products like the iris scanner now have to hand over the ropes to the new team. Sabrina Eros struggles to hand over the decision-making authority to the team. She perceives this as losing control over the whole development process. Now, trusting this Scrum Team that has never worked together feels scary. Roy is a great guy but doesn't always seem as consistent as needed. Also, the fact that the scope isn't very clearly defined upfront doesn't help navigate in uncertain times. And why would they not just leverage Sabrina's experience as a project manager? She knows exactly how this will go down the line. She will have to manage everything, hire more people when the project is running late, and then she'll have to report everything and take the blame in front of higher management. She's already *not* looking forward to that.

Roy keeps her close and informs her frequently so she can tell him what she wants. As managers are a form of stakeholders, too, he thinks it's better to keep them happy. Before starting the Sprint, Roy and Sabrina decide they'll need an extra preparation period to define the Product Backlog in detail so that the developers will know exactly what to do. A so-called Sprint 0 to ensure everything is set in place. The rest of the Scrum Team is frustrated by the delayed start, but they can do nothing about it now. Management decides that they will have to go with it. Together, they create the backlog.

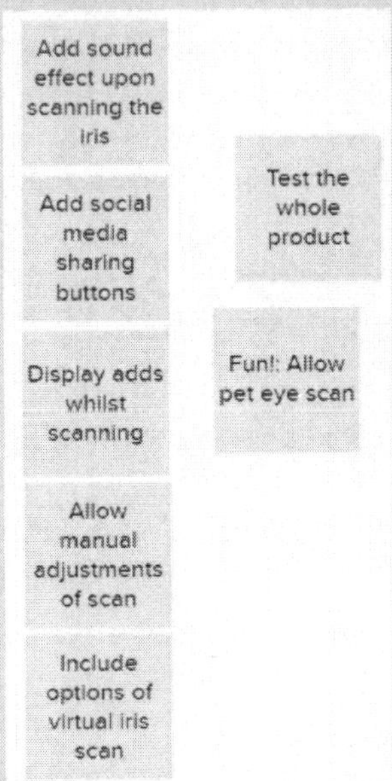

Figure 5 - Terrible example of Product Backlog Items for an iris scanner.

Sabrina suggests, "Let's put this into JIRA as soon as possible so we can add full details for every step. That way, we'll make it easier to understand what they need to build." Jax overhears the discussion and has a mild stroke. He decides not to do anything about it yet, as political influence is too strong at this point. There are bigger fish to fry first. Changing everything at once might cause resistance and lower buy-in.

One of those bigger fish is ensuring that the Sprint Planning event occurs. Jax, as an experienced Scrum Master, plans for eight hours. The duration of the Sprint has yet to be decided, and this first event will provide the perfect opportunity to do so. Within seconds after sending the invitation to the rest of the team, the first response comes back.

"Why on earth is this planned for that long? That must be a joke, right? We're all experienced people; we know how this stuff works." Johanna doesn't hide her frustration.

"Well," Jax replies, "the timebox of the Sprint Planning event is eight hours, and we don't have anything refined, planned, or done yet. We need to go through many things, so let's take the time to do that properly. It's just going to save us time down the road."

Reluctantly, she accepts the invitation. But before doing so, a proper kick-off is needed. Management brings in pizza, and even the CEO, John Ira, comes in to give a short speech.

"Guys, as you all know, this is an incredibly important project. The future of the company and the job security of many people in it depend on the outcomes of your work. We brought in this lovely pizza to make it a great start and as a token of our appreciation. It will not be easy, but I'm confident we have the right people on board to get the job done. You guys will save us tons of money and speed up delivery. We expect you to complete this by the year's end."

John meant it with all the positivity in the world, but he can't prevent his message from missing the impact as intended. The team feels enormous amounts of pressure to uphold the life quality of their colleagues, as well as ensure a healthy company. Especially considering that it's now late March, meaning they have nine months left to deliver a completely new and complex product with a framework that only Jax is familiar with. The kick-off was intended to be uplifting and generate a positive spirit at the start of the development, but it did quite the opposite. What if they don't make it? What if this project fails? All of it would be on their conscience to carry. This kick-off only elevates the fear of failing.

Being the Scrum Master, Jax is looked upon to solve these issues. He should be the one upholding Scrum, so the glorious task of being the fixer of everything John just destroyed is laid in his hands. Confused and concerned team members expect him to tell them precisely what to do to achieve their goals. But right now, the only goal the team has is to keep the quality of life for their colleagues stable and ensure that the company doesn't go bankrupt. Neither of these say anything about what kind of value is supposed to be delivered on the side of the product. *That's going to be the first challenge to tackle...* Jax thinks.

<u>*Where do we go from here?*</u>

Chaos, like in the case of Roy and Sabrina, is not uncommon. In full transparency, we see this in many organizations when the change in the ways of working is not thoroughly discussed. Many buzzwords are thrown around, but the true essence of change is not embedded or understood. Change is included in those buzzwords. It's mentioned so often that it almost feels like the whole world will be different tomorrow. And *that* is where the issue lies for many. More on that later.

The intention behind words is essential. John could have shared the most beautiful words, the bravest story, or the most cunning vision; but if there is no sincerity in his words, or he doesn't truly stand behind them, a tiny seed of doubt is planted in the receivers of his words. Seeds that often suffer from confirmation bias. It is found that our brain initially believes the words but has a self-generated doubt based on knowledge and experience.[12] How can we expect others to follow

[12] *Asp, et al, "A Neuropsychological Test of Belief and Doubt: Misleading Damage to Ventromedial Prefrontal Cortex Increases Credulity for Misleading Advertising"," PMC3391647, Front Neurosci (07/09/2012):, 10.3389/fnins.2012.00100*

if the ones deciding on change don't believe it themselves? This is where narratives and understanding come into play. A shared understanding is crucial in a world where technological advances follow up at a high pace, affecting our day-to-day business. We've heard people state they experience "change fatigue." This lack of shared understanding can hinder the start of change.

One of the most often used words with vastly different understandings is "value." We want to increase value, so, let's try to unravel it.

Beauty is in the Eyes of the Beholder

Or, as Dr. Phil used to say in his shows: *"Perception is reality."* Putting these words in the context of product delivery, there is no single way of determining what value means. Value is a highly subjective thing, and understanding this subjectivity is crucial. If we asked five different people what value means to them, we would get five different answers. Yet, in Scrum, we are there to deliver value. Value is delivered by bringing Done Increments to production. That's the only measure of progress, as there is no useful way to measure whether a Scrum Team has created something that satisfied the needs of the stakeholders when it's not in production yet.

Increments are new pieces of working product combined with all other previous increments. They are not stand-alone; the collection of increments work together and complement each other. Look at it as a puzzle versus a stack of squares lying side by side. A puzzle connects the pieces and ultimately forms a single product. There are no side pieces of the puzzle, only the entire image. You might get the same image with stand-alone pieces like the side-by-side squares, but messing that image up doesn't require much effort. They're not connected; they only appear to be when looking at it from a distance.

Value can have different forms. A few examples:

- **Happiness.** Happiness, too, is subjective. Kids might be overjoyed by obtaining the latest and greatest Pokémon game; others are delighted by a new washing machine (a true sign of me getting older – Sander). But it can be more abstract than that. The entertainment industry thrives on the happiness levels of others. Music festivals, Formula 1 races, and NFL matches relate to the observer's happiness. After all, it's the happiness of the viewers that brings in the money for the performers. And with happiness, we don't mean that people are always over the moon with everything; the sheer entertainment football matches bring, for instance, is a form of happiness, too.

There's a darker side to happiness as well. Remember the mobile game *Flappy Bird?*[13] The game itself provided entertainment to the users. Ten million downloads within twenty-two hours is a big feat. People were losing their minds over the game's popularity, but it was a frustrating experience for many when they couldn't win. Even though the developer of the game, Dong Nguyen, earned $50k per day, he was far from happy.[14] Complaints, threats, and people begging him for money were the result of the success he experienced, which initially seemed to bring a lot of happiness. The reversed version of the proverbial "one man's trash is another man's treasure."

- **Financial Value:** Continuing the previous example, money can be seen as a value point. It is vital to sustain a healthy cash flow when working for an organization. The traditional cash cow is an example of a successful product that provides a significant chunk of revenue.
  Examples of extremely successful products upon release:

    - Coca Cola
    - Nike Air Jordan
    - Nintendo Wii
    - Instagram

  Don't be discouraged if your product doesn't appear on this list. According to the late Dr. Clay Christensen, 95% of 310,000 new products fail.[15]
- **Broader Societal Benefits:** Not expressed in financial gains per se, but the benefit to society is a form of value in and of itself. A great example of a company that has become successful this way is The Ocean Cleanup. Dutch founder Boyan Slat created an autonomous, floating device that takes out trash from rivers and oceans and puts it into an accompanying trash vehicle. At the time of writing this, a total of 1.747.409kg has been removed so far, leading to healthier habitats for animals and cleaner

[13] *https://en.wikipedia.org/wiki/Flappy_Bird*

[14] *https://www.rollingstone.com/culture/culture-news/the-flight-of-the-birdman-flappy-bird-creator-dong-nguyen-speaks-out-112457/*

[15] *https://www.inc.com/marc-emmer/95-percent-of-new-products-fail-here-are-6-steps-to-make-sure-yours-dont.html*

water to drink. With a highly tangible goal ("Our aim is to have removed 90% of floating ocean plastic by 2040"), they strive to put themselves out of business once their job is done.

As these examples display, value is not a single thing. It depends on a multitude of factors. Yet many teams we have worked with haven't the slightest clue of what value means in their context. Oddly enough, embracing that you will not always be able to deliver value on the first try can be a critical factor for later success. Due to all the variables Scrum Teams work with, chances are that finding the right option on the first go are slim to none. Take Pixar's *Up*, the famous movie about an elderly widower who meets a boy scout on a mission who goes on unexpected adventures. The version that the broad audience has seen vastly differs from other versions in development. A particular culture needs to be relished to get to such a point. Pixar Studio is known for its *fail often, fail fast* mentality.

Ed Catmull, president at Pixar Animation Studios and Walt Disney Animation Studios, said: *"If you're able to at least realize academically that [failure is] two different things, then you realize that failure is a necessary consequence of doing something new."*

He meant that employees should be allowed to fail, try new ideas, and not judge the results. Unfortunately, no one has a crystal ball that will enable them to see the future. People need to feel safe and protected because they will not have to fear repercussions when things don't pan out the way they would have wanted right away.

Is it Done Yet?

One of the most common questions asked of all of our Scrum Teams is, "When will it be done?" That is a fair question, to be honest. Stakeholders invest their money in the product the team is building, so they want to know when to expect some ROI. The answer to this question isn't as easy to answer due to the complexity we're dealing with. Providing your stakeholders with a single date would prove to be incorrect. Roy's team will demonstrate the answer to this question later, as their stakeholders also need to know this. First, we need to address what we mean when things are done.

Done signifies some end state, even if that is for minimal work. This all goes back to one single sentence in the Scrum Guide that makes this so important:

"The entire Scrum Team is accountable for creating a valuable, useful Increment every Sprint."

Every Sprint? Surely not! We're not able to do that! We're paraphrasing here, but this is the regular sentiment we get when stating this. If we can't get a single piece of work, not even the smallest, into such a state that we could go to production if we decide to, this would be great material for reflection.

The crux is in two words:

- Valuable;
- Useful.

Perceptions of both can be vastly different from person to person. An Increment can be helpful without adding much value, and vice versa. Knowing if and when something is valuable means that there is a goal that needs to be accomplished. This could be anything that is a positive result of the value stakeholders derive from the product the Scrum Team builds. The scenario of Roy's team didn't show any clear sign of having a goal related to the product other than ensuring that people wouldn't get laid off. This doesn't say anything about the product's effect or how it will affect its users. The later vision is clear, and now it's time to think of the first possible steppingstone this team can create to start moving in that direction.

Scrum uses Sprint Goals to guide teams along the Sprint. Here are some bad versus good examples:

Bad examples	Good examples
Improve dashboard performance.	Improve dashboard loading speed by 30%.
Elevate Netflix onboarding.	Streamline Netflix onboarding journey to improve the satisfaction rate with >=25%.
Deliver User Story X, Y, Z.	Learn how features A and B affect the user interaction with the interface.

Sprint Goals create consistency and focus on the short-term objective. This gives the Scrum Team something tangible to plan against. Often, work not needed right now is pulled into the Sprint Backlog solely because a stakeholder says he needs this yesterday.

Picture this highly realistic scenario. Harry Potter (yes, this is what we're gonna go with) is fighting an epic (not the JIRA one) battle with Voldemort. It's a life-or-death scenario. Beating Voldy is the most essential thing right now. Then, all of a sudden, Ginny Weasley comes in to ask Harry a trivial question that is entirely unrelated to the battle he's fighting at that very moment. Harry's not going to stop blasting away at Voldemort; else he will not be able to achieve his Sprint Goal of "Defeat Voldemort with at least X amount of life left so that I will not be hospitalized for more than two weeks." We're confident you can picture the confusion on Harry's and even Voldemort's faces in this scenario. Believe me, we're just as confused when we see the Scrum Team pick up completely unrelated work without proper reasoning. Below are some possible correct answers when Ginny (stakeholder) approaches your team with additional work.

Figure 6 - While trying to achieve his goal, Harry gets interrupted by a stakeholder.

Harry Potter scenario	Scrum scenario
What the ... Can't you see I'm fighting a different battle here?! Go and see Dumbledore!	Developers: *We're sorry, but this isn't related to our current Sprint Goal and is not production-interrupting, so please talk to the Product Owner.*

*F*** yes, Ginny, this will help me beat him!*	*This will accelerate our delivery and learning; we will jump on this immediately.*
Dumbledore: *Aaah, very well, young Weasley; we shall execute this next semester. 40 Story Points to Gryffindor!*	Product Owner: *This could be useful, but not right now. I will order it correctly into the Product Backlog.*
Harry: *Never!*	Scrum Team: *Never!*

The moral of this story is that not creating a focus on what matters most right now and could deliver the most value right now with an eye on moving in the direction of the Product Goal(s) and Vision allows for waste to increase in the system. The Product Backlog will be bloated with useless and unsupportive Items (also called Marshmallow Backlogs).

Formulate a Sprint Goal with your Scrum Team that allows for creative thinking. None of the example goals mention anything about *how* to build that goal, only the desired and measurable outcome.

Planning for Increments

Let's dive a level deeper into what it means to be done. Being "Done" means no more work is left to perform before going to production. We could release this instance right away if we wanted to. No deploying to staging, no deploying to sandbox before heading to the hands of the customer, nothing. Some teams even decided to deploy to production before the Sprint Review and hide the new functionality behind a curtain called "feature toggles." Merely flipping the switch is sufficient to bring the latest work into the hands of their users.

Understanding what it means to be in a state of "Done" is essential. Stakeholders know what activities have been performed on the latest Increment, and developers know what activities to perform. This makes good input when planning the coming Sprint. This alignment on these activities creates a checklist that *has* to be performed at least before the end of the Sprint. The checklist is called the Definition of Done and cannot be downplayed. This relates to the two words mentioned earlier. Does an Increment hold value when the quality levels are below par? It might be helpful but might not hold the best value. Let's put that into a different perspective with a personal example by Sander, illustrating why this common understanding is important and what *technical debt* and *undone work* means.

The other day, I walked into my kitchen. My lovely kids had made a mess of it. It looked like a grenade exploded, and the perpetrators had fled the crime scene. Milk was over the floor and countertop, plates were on the stove, and cups were in the fruit bowl for God knows why. As the Developers of this less-than-lovely scenery were no longer present, I couldn't ask them why they used their decentralized decision-making powers to make these specific choices. Being the Product Owner in this case, I rallied the troops. Said troops rallied with a guilty look on their faces. This is a clear metric for me to work with. However, as will be discussed in this chapter, psychological safety is critical for people to thrive, so I ensured that this terrible decision-making is non-punishable and that they are okay with perceived failure. After talking to them, I realized I was partly to blame, as I didn't provide a clear goal. They were developing whatever they were developing—pancakes, sandwiches, a fancy new piece of hardware that cleans their rooms, who knows. I didn't specify the goal that I wanted to have after they ran their experiments. So, I did.

"I want a nicely cleaned kitchen so I won't break my neck when I walk into it. This means that I don't want to see any oceans of milk anymore, I don't want to see that demolition area on the counter, and I don't think cups qualify as fruit. Would like to have them gone, too." A certain sense of drama never was one of my lacking talents.

So, a few moments later, I walked back into the kitchen to test the latest Increment, and voila, everything was gone! It looked spotless(ish)! Fantastic job, Developers; off you go to play. A few minutes later, when I wanted to get a cup of tea, a bunch of cups fell out of the cupboard upon opening, and plates were thrown in as if they were frisbees. The paper towels were flown into the otherwise organized cupboard. Again, it was a reflection moment for me. Even though I have stated the end goal, we never discussed the quality standards as a team. To me personally, they were obvious. My sweet developers had a very different idea. This created a big pile of ***technical debt***, corner-cutting, or the making of poor decisions to release the latest Increment to production sooner. In this case, the Increment I received looked terrific on the outside. Looking under the hood, it was a complete mess. Was it useful? Yes, to a certain extent. Was it valuable? Not so much. Sometimes, it can make sense to release an Increment with technical debt, but that will be discussed later in this book.

Undone work means you cannot go to production whatsoever. To stick to my kitchen example, imagine you have chosen to get a new one installed. You've been anticipating starting to cook with that new centerpiece of the house, as your previous Carrara countertop didn't cope well with the pasta stains. The installers call you at work to say they are done and ready for usage. It is in production. Yet when you arrive back home, you get presented with a big hole where the oven is supposed to be, and there is no sign of a sink. It's unworkable: the work is undone without technical debt.

Activities that might go into your Definition of Done (DoD):

- Creating or updating relevant documentation;
- Acceptance criteria are incorporated;
- Corporate designs are checked with legal;
- Spelling check performed;
- Integration tests have passed;
- Unit tests have passed;
- Regression tests have passed.

These are examples of prodcts where the direct impact of a lack of a Definition of Done is low, yet it can result in high reputational damage or, even worse, .5-star reviews on Yelp. But what if the product was something more lifesaving?

My Dad has a pacemaker. Imagine what would happen if there would have been no clear idea of what it means to have a valuable, useful Increment. What would happen if, for instance, testing was skipped? Or would the latest release notes have hampered surgeons from understanding certain areas of the product?

Team Dynamics Vary

Roy's team is off to a rough start. They haven't even begun development, and the expectations are sky-high. The business impact on the organization is clear now, but individual team members have never collaborated. They might be unsure of how they fit into the team, the effect on the overarching goal, or how well they will get along with one another. Throughout development, teams go through certain phases, or stages, as Bruce Tuckman[16] calls them. From uncertainty to friction to a semi-stable performance stage, every team goes through them somehow. It's not a chronological order either; teams can go back and forth between them. It's good to be aware of these stages, which are natural to experience. Each stage has its challenges and benefits. Note that there are many theories on group dynamics, and we have chosen this one to highlight, as it has been part of our development and growth in Scrum Teams and coaching.

First Stage: Forming

As mentioned in the paragraph above, people might feel unsure of their part in the team and its dynamics. They might be anxious, nervous, curious, or excited to start their new group. Leaders are essential in providing the new team with a direction and guiding them to start moving there. We've seen teams where people are leaning back and awaiting the challenges to be delivered on a silver platter; we've seen teams that can't wait to go to the bar together and get to know each other in an engaging environment.

Second Stage: Storming

In the Storming stage, people start pushing boundaries. This can be both good and bad; it's good to know where one can push those boundaries and how far one can go. On the other hand, friction between individuals is likely to arise, as preferred ways of working might not overlap. As with many elements in Scrum, inefficiencies will surface. It's up to the team to decide how to work with those and how to move forward.

We've never seen a team that had no disagreements or friction. If everything is always like Walhalla all the time, we would be freaked out and start poking around to break the surface tension. If handled well, disagreements become constructive, where people respect each other's viewpoints and try to grow collectively. When handled poorly, there might be destructive disagreement, resulting in the potential cracks in the team dynamics becoming even bigger. Frustration is likely felt when accountabilities, goals, or boundaries are unclear. How is this stage dealt with, and does it make or break a team?

[16] Tuckman, Bruce W (1965). "Developmental sequence in small groups". Psychological Bulletin. 63 (6): 384–399

Somewhere at an early stage in my career, I worked with a team that had two people who were always in a latent argument. It was never really outspoken, but you could feel it was there. At that point, I never had a good look into team dynamics and I was being dogmatic about Scrum. I wasn't equipped with the right tools to deal with this specific situation. If I had known about Tuckman's stages and the potential effect it could have at this specific stage, I would've recognized sooner that this was beyond my ability to resolve the situation at hand. Ultimately, the two had a big verbal fight in the middle of the office, and the situation was unfixable after that. Ironically, this was during a meeting where we just formed team agreements on how we work together. The agreements were broken before the ink had dried.

Third Stage: Norming

Assuming the situation above doesn't happen and people can start resolving their respective differences and appreciate the strong characteristics of the other, the team begins to get into a more harmonious dynamic. When past disagreements have been handled without too much impact on psychological safety, team members will be more comfortable opening up, asking for help, or admitting they made a mistake. A stronger bond starts to form, creating more commitment to the team's goals in the process.

Fourth Stage: Performing

Many people we spoke to said that a Scrum Team is expected to become high performing. Even though many don't have a clue what that entails, Scrum Teams reach this level at the *Performing* stage. Team members are truly cross-functional. Contradictory to popular belief that this means that one should be able to take over another in case of sudden disparity, cross-functionality means that the team possesses all the skills needed to create a useful, valuable Increment consistently.

Teams that have reached the *Performing* stage demonstrate the true meaning of cross-functionality. Individual members are more fluid role-wise. Adaptiveness in responsibilities is often seen, and differences among different members are used to optimize the team's performance as a whole.

Fifth Stage: Adjourning

Also referred to as the *Mourning* stage. In this stage, the client's needs have been fulfilled, the team gets disbanded, the project gets canceled, or individual members start working elsewhere (within the same organization or elsewhere). We have seen people who find this difficult stage, as the line between colleagues and friendship has become thin, and now they're broken up to work with different people. Others thrive on the challenges of a new team and new people. Be aware that even people seemingly okay at this stage might be impacted in a way they're not demonstrating. *Adjourning* as a team might require a different approach as a way of formal closure.

As with many other principles discussed so far, this book presents these stages in the case of Magnum Opus, as we have experienced these situations in practice.

Creating an Environment to Thrive In

Long have organizations fought mental battles with legacy mindsets created by Taylorism, Fordism, and many isms that have overstayed their welcome in complex environments. Modern-day complexity in work environments does not match this hierarchy-driven, if-this-than-that management style. You present me with X amount of work done; I present you with a paycheck. This works in organizations where expected results are straightforward to achieve, but those types of organizations are becoming less and less common.

There is a caveat: changing this one day over the other is nearly impossible. The majority of current managers have been educated with legacy ideas. Organizational culture cannot change as rapidly as you might hope. A few factors come into play in changing culture, of which the *gravity trap* is one that we see recurring most often. As if gravity is pulling them back, people revert to old behavior before they escape orbit and can go wherever they need. It takes persistence to instill improvement. The bigger the organization, the harder it is to change its culture.

I have a confession to make. I am a recovered management basher. I used to blame management for their inability to change or embrace the agile mindset as a whole. Then, one day, I was recording an episode of the Mastering Agility podcast with product development guru Jeff Gothelf, where he told me to remember that ever since the beginning of the Industrial Revolution, universities and other educators have been training managers to micro-manage. To look over people's shoulders and correct whatever they do wrong in their eyes. The empirical approach has not been part of our educational system until recently. Hence, we cannot blame them solely. Frequently, they're not being provided the means to harness change themselves, and they keep on doing what they feel is best given the circumstances. Managers need support to become the leaders they need to be. My viewpoint changed ever since.

This book doesn't cover a guide to changing an entire conglomerate organization. To learn more about that, we would like to refer to Steven Kotler's *The Art of Impossible.* To reduce complexity and maintain relatability, this book focuses on changing the people involved in building a complex product in close and semi-close proximity.

Like any change (for instance, Sander's endless road to get in shape), changing culture takes time, effort, and perseverance. The journey will have many ups and downs, but it pays off down the road. We were inclined to write "pays off at the end," but we like to remind ourselves, and you, dear reader, that agility has no end state. It is a constant evolution led by emergent insights. It is a journey with no linear line toward the desired state, yet it has many ups and downs, back and forth, yays and nays. As with product development, it helps to have a desired state in mind. What do the organizations that we want look like? Where are we currently? What is the smallest thing we can change *right now* to be better than yesterday?

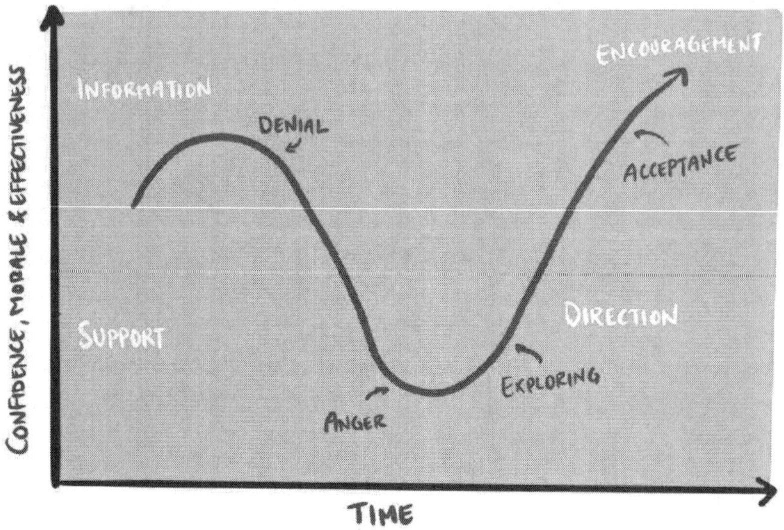

Figure 7 - The road is long and not straightforward.

Although every organization is unique and requires a unique approach to change, there is one universal similarity: without instilling psychological safety, results would be limited at best and nullified at worst. Again, leaders need to display the behavior and characteristics they expect others to bring to the changing organization. Embodying these changes means leading by example, acting as catalysts for others to follow, and empowering them to do the same.

Little things are more powerful than leaders speaking up about their challenges and how they feel about them. Admitting you don't know something or that you're anxious about the changes helps others be open about how they feel and what their needs are. This transparency provides direction to support the agile transition. In the case of Magnum Opus, John Ira attempted to show his leadership style but did more harm than good. He started by seemingly understanding the challenges and the position they were in but then made a U-turn by putting all that pressure on the shoulders of the team members instead of making it a collaborative effort. A disbalance is created, making Roy and his cohorts less likely to speak up. A downward spiral forms, making a self-fulfilling prophecy of not achieving their goals more likely.

Traditional management methods can be misused to create FDD (Fear Driven Development). Signs of an FDD organization:

- Highly political tactics – you scratch my back, I'll scratch yours;
- Development purely incentivized with money;
- People are holding back new ideas out of fear of other people stealing their potential success;
- Speaking the hard truth is not appreciated;
- No job security;
- Lots of gossiping;
- Promotion is based on your ability to walk in line;
- People are being treated as resources.

Note that we left these bullet points blank so you can check the boxes that pertain to your organization.

"For knowledge work to flourish, the workplace must be one where people feel able to share their knowledge! This means sharing concerns, questions, mistakes, and half-formed ideas."

— Amy C. Edmondson, *The Fearless Organization: Creating Psychological Safety in the Workplace for Learning, Innovation, and Growth*

Without Trust, No Team

In our experience, the most misinterpreted or misunderstood aspects of Scrum are the Scrum Values. A group of individuals working simultaneously does not make a team. It's trust that forms the glue between them. Trust is created by enacting the Scrum Values, easily remembered by the acronym FORCC (or FOCCR, whatever resonates better with you). The letters stand for:

- Focus;
- Openness;
- Courage;
- Commitment;
- Respect.

These serve as a guideline, not a hard "thy shall now respect thy teammates because I tell you so." Be aware that without trust, it becomes increasingly more challenging to be transparent and perform proper inspection and adaptation. An extreme example is the United States Navy SEALs. Navy SEALs know that things could hit the fan when they get deployed. They are not commonly being requested to guide traffic at your local elderly retirement home, for instance. When they get deployed, they might not make it back. They have to be 100% sure that the people they are on a mission with will do everything in their power to ensure they and their teammates will return to their loved ones. If there's only one in the team who only slightly thinks, "See Billy over there, I don't really trust him," the entire team folds like a house of cards. Even though the impact on the Scrum Team differs from that of the Navy SEALs, trust still works similarly. In his book *The Infinite Game*, Simon Sinek talks about this group of elite men and women,[17] where he shows that they prefer someone with a high level of trust and medium performance over someone with medium trust and high performance.

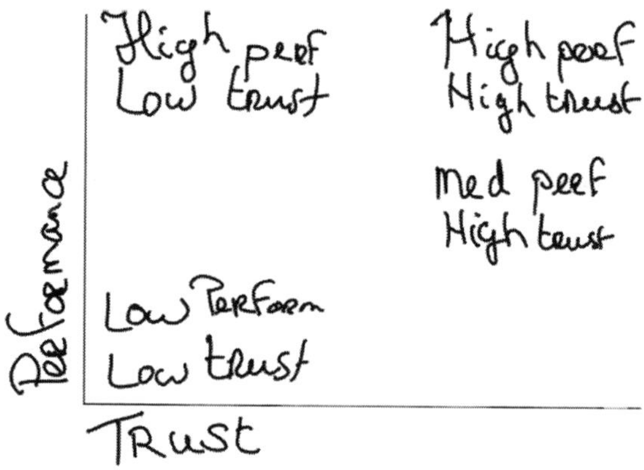

Figure 8 - Trust says more about your ability as a team player than your performance.

The Choices of a Scrum Master

In our experience, Scrum Master accountability is misunderstood. Scrum Masters are empowered to work with developers, Product Owners, and the broader organization. Quite frequently, we see Scrum Masters who are almost forced to remain within the Scrum Team's boundaries, limiting the potential Scrum Masters could unlock for the broader environment. To support the application of the proper leadership Scrum Masters bring, we need a deeper understanding of what areas of choice could be made to take on specific challenges.

[17] Sinek, The Infinite Game (Penguin Books Ltd, 2020)

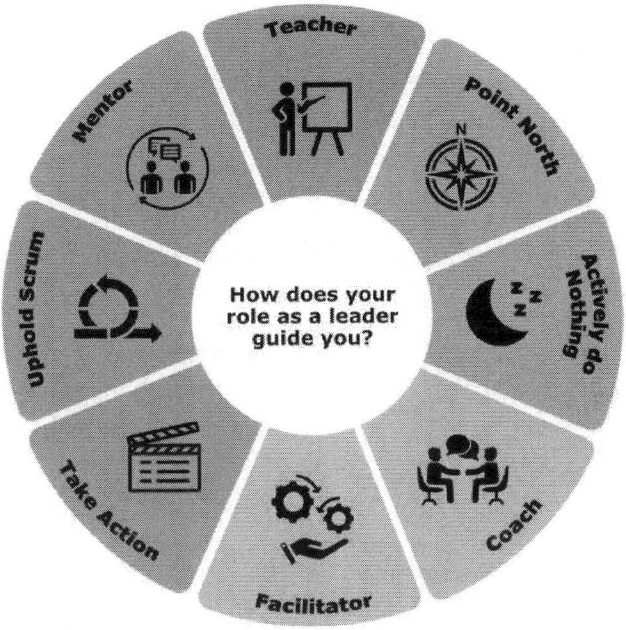

Figure 9 - The Choices of a Scrum Master.

What? Scrum Masters do more than facilitate? We can only picture jaws dropping to the floor and massive head-scratching while looking at this wheel. Yet it is true; here, we have the corporate equivalent of a Swiss pocketknife. What to apply when, and when to take what choice is never easy, nor will it be done perfectly. It requires situational awareness to feel the impact of each choice. Often, time is limited to making confident choices, so these must become ingrained in day-to-day work. Practice them. Reflect on them. See what to improve in case a similar future case presents itself.

Teacher: Convey the message to the audience. Teach your Scrum Team, stakeholders, and organization how the Scrum framework works and how to apply the empirical approach. Different facilitation techniques often benefit teaching.

Mentor: As more experience is gained, the mentor choice often becomes more prevalent. It is vital to use your experience and knowledge to support the growth of less experienced Scrum Masters.

Facilitator: A neutral stance that helps a group collaborate better, achieve goals, or make decisions. Various techniques are applied, for instance, those coming from Training from the Back of the Room[18] or Liberating Structures.[19]

Coach: A coach provides guidance to someone so that they can achieve their goals and reach their full potential. Unlike a mentor, who shares knowledge, skills, and experience, the coach is not about providing answers but about having the coachee think about their process and challenges.

Upholding Scrum: Ensuring that Scrum is applied as it is meant to be applied, preventing mechanical or "Zombie" Scrum.

Actively do nothing: Although kicking back on the beach of Bonaire sounds like the perfect Actively Do Nothing choice, that is not what we mean here. Purposely keeping a little distance to inspect what might unravel or how the rest of the Scrum Team might pick up its ability to self-manage is sometimes needed for the Scrum Team's growth. Answering challenges might seem helpful, but sometimes, others should figure out their own path.

Take action: Opposite to the previous choice, sometimes it is necessary to step in and say, "Here's what we're gonna do," when conflict becomes destructive over constructive, when people get hurt, when unethical behavior is displayed, to name a few situations. Don't be too eager here. Ask questions over taking action first.

Point North: Ensuring people are on the same page and communicating goals. This doesn't mean communicating these goals yourself per se, but making sure that they happen. The Product Owner remains accountable for sharing the goals related to the product, whereas Scrum Masters could reiterate the goals when working as a team.

As is evident, there is a lot more to being a great Scrum Master than the default facilitator that many believe it to be. Apply these choices to all levels of the organization, and you have a powerful change agent to relish. Empowering these change agents to do what they need to do genuinely can prevent poor choices not in line with proper Scrum, like starting Sprint 0 – an untimeboxed period before the first Sprint where work gets prepared for the Scrum Team to pick up. Planning

[18] *Sharon L. Bowman, Training From the Back of the Room!(Jossey-Bass Inc. U.S.), 2009*

[19] *Lipmanowicz and McCandless, The Surprising Power of Liberating Structures: Simple Rules to Unleash a Culture of Innovation (Heart Media), 2014*

for more certainty is only a symptom of comfortability while dealing with complexity.

The Choices of a Product Owner

Product Ownership is not a straightforward job. Accountable for maximizing the value derived from the product, Product Owners have to continuously balance their options, decide what to do, and, maybe even more importantly, what not to do. In their daily work, they talk to hordes of people, look at piles of data, and try to satisfy everyone's needs (preferably yesterday). To support the empirical challenge of a Product Owner, certain choices could be made to pave the way forward.

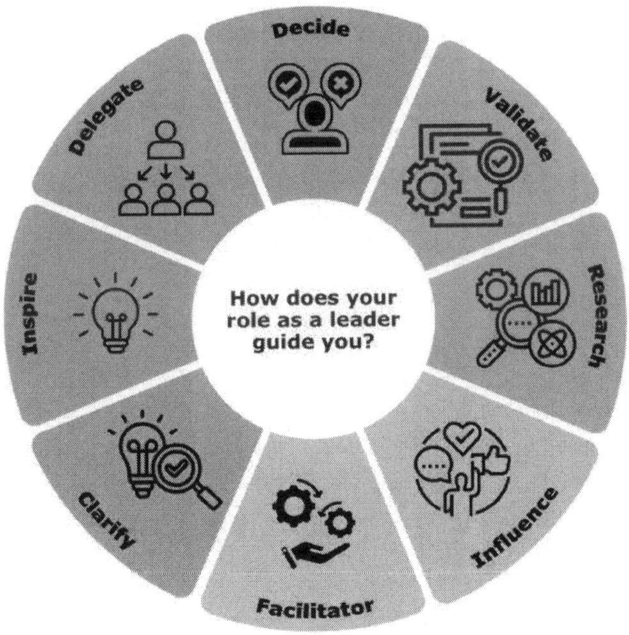

Figure 10 - The Choices of a Product Owner.

Decide: The entire organization must respect the choices made by the Product Owner. The Product Owner is empowered with the decision-making authority on *all* aspects of the product, including the release schedule, budget, ordering the backlog, architecture, and technology.

Delegate: Product Owners may decide to delegate certain choices to others in the Scrum Team so that they can focus on more urgent matters, such as ordering the

Product Backlog or deployment choices. Would it be a good idea to delegate budgetary or release schedule decisions? Probably not. Ultimately, the Product Owner is still accountable for the effects of delegating.

Inspire: Understand why the work being performed matters and what direction the Scrum Team is heading. What kind of goals are we trying to achieve? Product Owners need to make sure everyone involved understands where we're going and why it's important.

Clarify: Substantiating certain choices or providing the developers with the right amount of information on Product Backlog Items is key to ensuring valuable, useful Increments are being built. Lack of details only prolongs cycle time, creates confusion, and frustrates.

Research: Research (potentially new) markets, personas, and technology for your product to thrive. What are the pains and gains of our target audience? Could we use this product in different areas? How could new technology like Chat GPT impact our product? Researching data, both direct (usage index, ROI, cycle time) and indirect (employee happiness, customer satisfaction). The results of this research can be used for decision-making.

Validate: Validate how the Scrum Team's work is adding value. Define hypotheses. Release early and often. Shorten the feedback loop. Compare the outcomes to the hypotheses and respond to learnings quickly.

Facilitate: Hold on, didn't we just see this at the Scrum Master's choices? Correct! That doesn't mean that the Scrum Master is the only one who should be able to facilitate. We would argue that facilitation skills for Product Owners are equally important. Facilitating Sprint Reviews, problem-solving workshops, or experimentation events can bring valuable insights.

Influence: Influencing stakeholders or people who could support your product smooths the process of value delivery. Navigating the political landscape or gathering investors requires high people smarts and proficiency in the product domain.

Gauging when to apply what activity and to what degree is like a dance. It's never stationary; it's constantly in a delicate motion. Focus too much on one of these eight, and you'll neglect other areas. Remaining too generic will lead to a lack of deepened knowledge and skills. There is never an entire day where the Product Owner applies just one of these choices. When a Product Owner who applies these choices closely collaborates with the Scrum Master, a dynamic duo is born. Corporate Batman and Robin are here to fight plateaus in development.

Kicking off a change in ways of working vastly different from before requires proper scoping, the right tone, and often not saying many things. Refrain from saying things like "no one has to fear for their jobs" or similar messages if people don't want to be afraid of it. It's counterproductive. When people talk about the event later, they might not fully remember it correctly or think it's not true.

Person A: *"Did you hear what he said about fearing for our jobs?"*

Person B: *"Yeah, we don't need to fear losing our jobs. But apparently, they did think about it..."*

Person A: *"What if this just sets the stage for later layoffs?"*

Let's try that differently. We explicitly ask you *not* to think about a blue horse with purple wings dancing before a paper Kanban board. What are you thinking about right now? Probably that blue horse.

Use the lessons in this chapter to set yourself up for success. Having everyone on the same page from the start prevents friction at later stages of development. If you are reading this and in charge of the budget, read this as "could save me a ton of money on coaching down the line."

Ryan and Sander's Summary Feed (RSS Feed)

If there are any points that we want you to take away from this chapter, they are as follows:

- There is no single answer to the definition of value. Everyone has a different view on what they feel adds value to their lives. Creating alignment on expected outcomes is essential.
- Transparency about when work is truly done and ready to go into the hands of the user is needed to understand what needs to be performed during a Sprint.
- Any team goes through different stages of development. Recognizing and understanding these helps provide adequate support for the team's growth.
- It is normal for people to feel all kinds of emotions while the team goes through stages. It's *not* normal to lack emotion, and it is usually a sign of an underlying issue.
- Psychological safety is needed for knowledge workers to speak up and create an environment where innovation can thrive.
- Every accountability is unique and does not have a day-to-day agenda that is the same throughout. Understanding what kind of choices accompany each accountability helps maximize efficacy.

Reflection

Use this page to reflect on the initial questions at the beginning of this chapter and what you may have uncovered throughout.

How do you define value in your situation? Would your stakeholders agree with this description?

Is your product team working as a team or as a group of individuals? What could be the most impactful improvement?

If you're a Product Owner or a Scrum Master, which of these stances are your strengths and which need more attention?

3.

Planning for Value

"Give me six hours to chop down a tree, and I will spend the first four sharpening the axe."

– Abraham Lincoln

Preflective Questions

In our quest to maximize value, we must pause and reflect on our current strategies and practices. We frequently set ambitious targets like "Increase efficiency by X" or "Enhance customer satisfaction significantly." These goals are great, but we often feel lost when questioned about our existing baseline. For example, what is our current level of efficiency? So, how can we gauge improvement without knowing where we stand? Wanting progress to be visible is natural; we strive to excel, innovate, and outperform continuously. However, without a clear starting point, our efforts may be wasted if we lose sight of tangible progress.

What would their biggest concerns be if your team used Scrum for the first time tomorrow morning?

From the organization's perspective, what quantitative benefits will they expect from a Scrum team?

As the Scrum Master, how could you empirically prove your value?

Today is the day. It's the first day of Sprint 1 for Roy's new Scrum Team. People are apprehensive, but not Roy. He's been dreaming about turning this company around for so long. From what he's read on LinkedIn, Scrum will answer all their problems. With Sprint Planning happening soon, he really believes that the company will start to turn around.

At ten a.m., the team moves to the meeting room where Sprint Planning is scheduled. The Developers are indifferent because, from what they've heard Jax saying, they're confident that Scrum will give them nothing more than their current process, but they are willing to give it a try. As they sit down to begin the event, one of them even says,

"Oh, let's just get this over with so we can get back to work."

But there's a problem.

"Where is Roy? Where is our Product Owner?" Jax says.

He decides to go and look for Roy and quickly finds him grabbing a fresh cup of tea and chatting to some of his colleagues.

"Do you realize we're in Sprint Planning waiting for you, Roy?" Jax asks him abruptly.

"Yes, yes, I'm coming. I was having a conversation with these stakeholders," Roy replies, quickly shuffling a pile of sticky notes into his notepad.

Fifteen minutes after the scheduled start time, Roy and Jax finally walk into the room. Roy doesn't apologize, and you can tell that the Developers are frustrated at being made to wait around. What makes it even worse is that Roy has a proud look on his face. The stack of sticky notes that Jax saw earlier is ceremoniously removed from his notepad. He starts shuffling through them.

"I've been thinking about what I want you to work on over the next few weeks. Here you go." Roy says this as he hands the documents to the Developers around the table.

"The sticky note you've got is what I want you to work on over the next few weeks. That's your Sprint Goal," he says as he takes his seat.

The developer's faces drop. Jax can see that they all think, "Here we go again."

Jax decides to challenge Roy on his approach.

"It's great that you're thinking about a Sprint Goal, Roy, but do you remember when we spoke about there being one single Sprint Goal per Sprint? In my experience, when a team focuses on one thing at a time, they are more likely to deliver it. That means we are more likely to give value to our stakeholders by the time the Sprint Review comes around. So, if you had to pick one of these sticky notes for the team to work on this Sprint, which would be it, Roy?"

"They're all important," he replies. "And I only handed out five sticky notes, so, with seven developers, we've got two people without anything to do. Plenty of capacity to do these things, I think."

The tension clearly begins to build between Jax and Roy because they start to raise their voices.

"It doesn't matter what you say, Jax. I've already committed to the stakeholders that all these things will be done. You saw me talking to them while getting tea before this meeting. They were really happy when I explained how much extra work Scrum will help us give them," Roy says defensively.

With the Developers now resigned to the fact that nothing has changed from how they used to work, any openness to using Scrum has now gone. They try to work with Roy, asking him what each of his sticky notes actually means. But unsurprisingly, Roy has no idea. At this point, Ronda challenges why he needs to learn about the stakeholders' problems.

"How can we fix these things if we don't know anything about the problems?" she says, as a proud smile appears on Jax, the Scrum Master's face.

"I haven't had any time, Ronda. I'm too busy with the other projects the organization needs me to work on. Anyway, it's the job of the Developers to find out exactly what's needed," Roy informs her.

After only fifteen minutes, Roy stands up and decides to add one more thing as he walks to the door.

"Right, I think we're all planned for the next two weeks. Jax, can you make sure you give me daily updates on the progress toward each of these five Sprint

Goals so that I can make sure my commitment to the stakeholders is being met?"

Roy then leaves Sprint Planning feeling incredibly happy with himself. After all, he'd spoken to stakeholders and found out what they actually wanted.

After only thirty minutes, the event ends, and the Developers return to their desks. Most of them carry the sticky note that Roy handed them as their Sprint Goal.

Where do we go from here?

Being part of a Sprint Planning event like the one described above is heartbreaking for the Developers and the Scrum Master, as well as for personified value and the organization. It creates such a distinct lack of care for the product and how people work that it easily meets the bar for being unprofessional. Although we have all been part of poorly facilitated planning sessions (perhaps even as the facilitator), for this to have taken place as the kickoff to Sprint 1 is hugely demoralizing for everyone taking part, perhaps except for Roy, who thought it went well. Breaking this story down into key takeaways is hard, but there are a few things that stand out:

- Roy is a responsive rather than proactive Product Owner. He has no understanding of the product's road map, leading to an unclear focus for the developers.
- Management, in the form of Roy and likely Sabrina, is expecting frequent updates regarding output instead of outcome. Specifically, he is asking Jax, the Scrum Master, to give him these updates.
- While efficient Sprint Planning can be an outcome of effective Product Backlog refinement, it was over rapidly due to a lack of transparency—there was no information for the Scrum Team even to discuss!

These three key areas are by no means the extent to which this Sprint Planning can be described as a car crash, but we'll review each of these in turn and discuss the impacts of their occurrence. Before we do, we encourage you to reflect on the three bullet points above and overlay your experience with them. If similar things have happened in the past with your Scrum Teams, what were the impacts?

Lack of a Product Roadmap

A Product Owner is accountable for maximizing the product's value. To do this, they need an understanding of where the product is and, more importantly, where they would like it to move. In Roy's case, it is not evident that he considered this. While you may argue that Roy has engaged with his stakeholders and gathered sticky notes on their problems, this is evidence of a responsive approach to Product Backlog management, so-called "firefighting."

Figure 11 - Product Owners shouldn't be handing out work.

Consider what Roy would have asked the developers to focus on if he hadn't bumped into the stakeholders while grabbing tea. When a Product Owner doesn't know where their product is heading (commonly expressed as a single Product Goal), they will end up with an incoherent, unstable product that offers limited value to the end users. Suppose the Product Owner is accountable for maximizing value. In that case, they need to know what value they aim for, simply because it is far more likely that value will be delivered when purposely planning toward it instead of randomly discovering it by luck.

With Magnum Opus, the lack of product direction is coupled with a distinct black hole of value metrics. They ostensibly have no way or aren't considering how they will judge the product's success. How is it fairing in the market? Are users receiving value from its existence? One of the first questions an experienced Product Owner will ask is, 'Does this product need to exist?' because if a product's value to the market isn't well understood or defined, justifying continued product development is a risk. Far too many teams that we've worked with take the approach that delivering new features, resolving bugs, and innovating the product determines value, but my challenge to them and you, as the reader of this book, is to prove it. Prove that your product is worth continued investment using metrics—now, there is a challenge you can present to your Product Owners!

A tangible first step toward being able to do this is to put in place automated metrics to determine which areas of your product are frequently used more than others. If you work in software development, an example of a free tool offering this information is Hotjar. Hotjar is a tool that can present heat maps (areas of frequent user activity) for any website that shows how users interact with your product (and even records their user experience in the form of videos for you to watch). Are they clicking on images, thinking that they are hyperlinks? Do they move off a particular page incredibly quickly, showing that it offers them little value? Scrum is based on empiricism, transparency, inspection, and adaptation, but bias often impacts inspection. While the Definition of Done helps to create a common language to remove some of this bias, quantitative metrics go one step further.

When working in the industry, one of the most common issues Scrum Teams face is to decide which metrics to gather. A small tip to help your teams move forward with this issue is to get them to role-play your customers. Some prompt questions that may help are:

- What makes you angry about this product? Is it system up-time, dead-links, support response time, bug frequency, etc.?
- What would increase your usage of this product? Is it data throughput, faster report generation, product load times, etc.?

The point here is to get them to consider product qualities (rather than development qualities) that the customer cares about. Gathering this kind of information demonstrates a mature Scrum Team. They have likely transitioned past output-based metrics (code coverage, cyclomatic complexity, the volume of product created, etc.) to outcome-based ones (click-through rate, net promoter score, number of successful merges). Whatever metrics you choose, ensure they are being gathered to inform decisions relevant to your product roadmap. This means that the metrics you gather may evolve and change over time depending on your Product Goal—collecting metrics (especially manually) is time-intensive and wasteful if they aren't used to make meaningful inspections that lead to timely adaptations. Importantly, however, when you obtain your metrics, you must be able to prove the value your product offers to the market. For example, you may begin seeing that metrics form part of Product Goals in the future.

Here are some examples of Product Goals that are driven by outcome-based metrics:

- 15% of our restaurant customers will leave us a 5* review on Trustpilot.
- We can successfully resolve 90% of support requests within seven days.

All of these Product Goals are informed and delivered by output. Still, the critical understanding here is that a product roadmap is focused on delivering an outcome for users instead of simply resolving the current fire—this is one of the things Roy needs to improve if the Scrum Team is to be successful in adopting Scrum.

Fundamentally, a product roadmap could have supported this Sprint Planning event by allowing the Developers to collaborate on formulating a single Sprint Goal. After all, a Sprint Goal is a tactical step toward an overarching piece of business value, and determining which Product Backlog items are needed is a vital requirement to form the Sprint Backlog.

An Update a Day Makes the Managers Go Away

Suppose we reflect on why Roy is asking for daily updates from the Scrum Master. In that case, he is likely doing so to either a) maintain some form of control over the progress of the Sprint, b) to avoid needing to be involved in discussion frequently with the developers, or c) to ensure that the commitments he made on behalf of the developers to the stakeholders are being met. Honestly, in our experience, it's probably all three.

I once worked with a client with an incredibly poor employee retention rate. They couldn't figure out why so many people were leaving (many were even refusing to take part in an exit interview)! I suggested (and for those who don't know me, I don't shy away from radical candor) that part of the problem was that commitments were being made to customers primarily by those who knew the least about the product (the very people I was speaking to at that moment). We discussed delocalized decision-making, empowered teams, and the impact of having commitments made on your behalf. They didn't get it... until I told them all I wanted a report on the value each product delivers by the end of the week – "I've told your senior managers to expect it." "That's ridiculous," they said. Then, as the saying goes, the penny dropped.

One of the many problems we see with teams being asked for frequent updates by their management is that they focus on doing more work over delivering more value. What we mean by this is that many organizations care about the volume of work being completed because that is (sadly) still the common understanding of how we maximize employee utilization. This approach fails to understand that output does not equal revenue generation—behavior change and customer sentiment do. For example, a Scrum Team could deliver ten Product Backlog items, yet only one may be valuable. All this goes to say that utilization is an incredibly poor measure of how a team is progressing during a Sprint—and yet this is exactly what Roy is asking for! If you have ever been in a similar situation where someone external to the Scrum Team asks for transactional updates, ask them what they intend to do with the information. Chances are, there will be nothing because they won't even understand it. Most managers we've worked with only understand the 'two states' of a Product Backlog item, done and not done, and this is absolutely okay. What is not okay is when they want to hear about the technicalities of turning requirements into a usable increment because, at that point, they are simply wasting time. **Unfortunately, these types of managers are still endemic in many organizations. As we progress through this book, you will probably start to personify Roy as a colleague you previously (or currently!) worked with, and that's okay with us. We permit you to imagine Roy as your own personal douchebag.**

Returning to our Sprint Planning story, do you remember who Roy requested updates from? That's right, Jax, the Scrum Master. The failed premise here is that the Scrum Master is in the position to offer these updates. The issue is twofold: firstly, the people who understand the real-term progress toward the Sprint Goal are the Developers themselves, and secondly, requesting updates from the Scrum Master implies that Jax is more senior than the rest of the Scrum Team. A successful Scrum Team relies on having zero hierarchy within the team; otherwise, demonstrating the Scrum values (particularly courage) is harder when you are required to challenge the opinion of someone senior.

Now, this isn't to say that people in organizations don't have more or less seniority than others—of course, they do, but how it manifests internally to the Scrum Team should be negligible. This is vital to the success of a self-managing team. If you were in the situation of Jax, how would you have responded to being asked to provide daily updates on the work of your colleagues? If Roy would like frequent updates concerning the Developers' progress, he could perhaps be encouraged to attend the Daily Scrum as a passive participant or even inspect the Sprint Backlog. You know, like the whole point of the artifact?

Let me tell you about a time when I was a Scrum Master for a team that used story points as their prime forecasting tool. There were two teams working on the same product: my team and another team in the same room. We chose to use story point values of 1, 2, 3, etc. and the other team chose to use 10, 20, 30, etc. When my team delivered 30 points during a Sprint, and the other team delivered 300, which team do you think the organization believed were being more effective? This is obviously a rhetorical question, but is also a sad indictment of organizations favoring output and specifically being blinded by the metrics in front of them. Maybe my team, with only 30 points output was delivering more value to the end users? Maybe the team who delivered 300 points was? The points are irrelevant, and that is one of the reasons why task-level updates to a Product Owner are ineffective.

Refinement as a Synonym for Transparency

Five sticky notes were written while grabbing a coffee. That's enough transparency, right? Roy certainly would think so, but we're not entirely sure the rest of the team would agree. Stakeholder feedback is one of the most important inputs when building a Product Backlog. To his credit, Roy did bring stakeholder feedback into Sprint Planning (however, this may have been obtained passively). The input of current market sentiment is incredibly important for a Scrum Team to decide what to tackle next. However, Roy was missing any further coherent ideas for the developers to discuss. As this was the first Sprint for this team, he had an excellent opportunity to work with them to use their expertise, coupled with the stakeholders' problems, to determine a valuable way forward tactically. Unfortunately, he took this opportunity to transactionally allocate work (and simultaneously remove any form of self-management) to the developers.

If he had used the sticky notes as a proposed input to the Sprint Backlog instead of its fixed scope, this whole event would likely have been much more successful. If only he'd been open to a bit of transparency. The concept of transparency comes down to three things: visibility (are people able to see the requirements and provide their feedback on them?), accessibility (are they written in such a way that people can inspect them?), and understanding. It is upon this final point of 'understanding' that transparency hinges. Suppose Developers, stakeholders, organizational managers, or anybody else inspecting the Product Backlog cannot understand the value a specific Product Backlog item offers. In that case, the Scrum Team is missing a possible opportunity for inspection and useful feedback. To share an example, which of these is easier to understand and provide feedback on?

- Place the .json structure into MongoDb after validating it with Prettify.

OR

- Our users can query data using simple search terms successfully.

There are a few points to highlight with the above two suggestions.

1. **Transparency is aided by behavior-oriented phrasing**

   When the Product Owner delegates responsibility to the developers to create Product Backlog items, they commonly phrase them in technical language that they are comfortable with. While the Product Owner is accountable for ensuring that Product Backlog items are communicated in such a way that they are transparent, it is very common for developers to be delegated some of the activity toward this. This can often lead to defining an upfront solution to inflexible work as they learn more thorough inspection (this is also one of the major problems of having a technically literate Product Owner). Additionally, users can't understand the value of an item like this and are therefore less enthusiastic about progress.

2. **Transparency is aided by an 'if this, then that' approach**

   What will your users be able to do once you deliver a specific Product Backlog item? Structuring your Product Backlog so that the user's desire is stated alongside how it will soon be manageable is vital to support empiricism. Why? Because this information is easier for someone to validate during a Sprint Review or even after release. From a developer perspective, this approach also encourages them to think more creatively instead of transactionally. This shift in mindset to end-user satisfaction can be a perfect trigger to move toward increased quality, frequent delivery, and genuine product ownership.

3. **A knowledgeable Product Owner aids transparency**

   It is perfectly possible to have transparent Product Backlog items that offer no value to the market. It all comes down to whether the Product Owner understands the customer. Have you ever heard your partner or friend say, 'I know you better than you know yourself'? Well, that is the job of a Product Owner—to know not just what the customers want now but to plan for what they will need in the future. When a domain expert guides the product, then communication efficiency (particularly around resolving developer questions) is improved. Minimizing guesswork enables the mitigation of risk.

If you want to improve transparency in your team, try inviting two or three representative users to an upcoming Sprint Planning event (perhaps those people Roy met while grabbing a coffee could have come along?). The purpose is not to scare the developers ("Eeeek, real people! Everybody run!") but rather to facilitate discussions that start with the ideal, non-technical solution to the problem, enabling impactful conversations that aim to solve customer issues. There is a common misconception in Scrum that where the Scrum Guide refers to 'inviting other people' to Sprint Planning, these are restricted to implementation-type people (technical experts that can guide developers on how to turn Product Backlog items into a usable increment), but that's simply not true. The first question we consider in Sprint Planning is 'Why?' And who better to answer this than some of the users themselves?

Some actionable ideas to try with your Scrum Team are:

- Select any Product Backlog item near the top and ask everyone (all three accountabilities) to write down what it will enable the user to do and how we will prove it added to the expected value. Shuffle them up and read them out. The purpose isn't to confuse but to address misconceptions.

- Whenever Product Backlog refinement is becoming too focused on the technical implementation, encourage someone to fulfill the 'Devil's Advocate' role to challenge proposals and promote external thinking. If done correctly, there will be a shift toward outcome-based discussions.

- Split-team refinement can help when attempting to refine disparate work threads. We accept that everyone can't be an expert in every area of the product. Still, by forming small sub-teams, even pairs, to refine (talk to the Product Owner, the users, and any external dependencies) in advance of Sprint Planning, you create experts who will create transparency by using the language of their peers.

Before we dive deeper into Sprint Planning and some of the other issues Roy's team faced, let's take an opportunity to reflect on them.

Describe the biggest failure in Sprint Planning that you have experienced recently.

What actions did you or the Scrum Team take in the moment to stay on track?

What actions did you or the Scrum Team take in the moment to stop it from recurring again in the future?

Review Roy's story again to determine which issues you've personally seen with your Scrum Team.

Let us guess: you skipped thinking about the previous questions, didn't you? If you didn't, please award yourself a gold star. If you did—we caught you! We told you this book would call you out and keep you on your toes! Reflection is a powerful activity we often don't get time to do, so take the opportunity when offered. Or not. It's your choice!

Issue After Issue After Issue

What else would you say went wrong in this Sprint Planning? If you're using this book as we intend, grab a highlighter and find anything you would challenge if it happened before you. When issues arise during Scrum events or just normal day-to-day, we need to be mindful not just of the immediate impact but also of tomorrow and the next day. What impact will allow this activity or comment to go unchallenged have on our future success? Every action that goes unchallenged gives the actor permission to repeat it, so being mindful of where you draw the line is an important professional reflection for us all to have.

Hindsight is a wonderful thing, though, and perhaps Jax wanted to challenge many of these approaches but couldn't. In the UK, there is a wonderful idiom of feeling like you're *'pissing into the wind,'* and we're sure that one doesn't need explaining. Could Jax have addressed the lack of courage to challenge Roy? The lack of technical planning to turn each sticky note into a Done increment? The lack of readiness for each of the sticky notes? Yes, but... sometimes you need to live to fight another day. Issue after issue after issue isn't just demoralizing for developers and anyone who cares about delivering quality work.

Successful Sprint Planning

Sprint Planning exists to answer three questions.

Why – Why are we expending effort on this Sprint? Why is the organization spending money on our team? Why does this product still exist?

What – What do we need to do to validate our 'why'? To do this, which Product Backlog items are required in our plan (Sprint Backlog)? What other work might we need to do during this Sprint?

How – How will we take this (hopefully) coherent set of requirements and turn them into a cohesive increment? How are we going to work together to achieve this?

These three questions drive everything in the Sprint Planning timebox, which is why immature Scrum Teams who think they can do it all in thirty minutes are lazy, lie to themselves, and have no idea what the stakeholders actually want, or all of these combined.

To improve Sprint Planning so that you can propose answers to these three questions, allow us to share some concrete techniques and actions that support self-management and empirical planning.

Allocation to Developers

How about just no? Any Scrum Master, Product Owner, or 'technical lead' who gives a Developer a piece of work to do (or worse still, inhumanely 'allocates' it to them in Jira...**shudders**) can stick that work right up their <insert appropriate orifice>. Scrum Teams work as a team, not as a collection of individuals. A common pattern is to encourage the most experienced Developer on a certain task to continue to do that work the next time it occurs. After all, that's efficiency, right? Well, no, it's not. There is no expectation that everyone is an expert in everything (which, incidentally, is one of the biggest misunderstandings of the term 'cross-functionality'). Still, there is an expectation that everyone is willing to muck in and give it a go. If Developers are simply passengers in Sprint Planning, something has gone horrifically wrong.

Remember, the Sprint Backlog is a plan for the developers; therefore, they should create it. If they aren't given the space to do that due to an overzealous Product Owner with a pile of sticky notes, then take the Product Owner and leave. Once the Sprint Goal is transparent, let the Developers know the Product Owner is available for clarification questions and then walk out; let them know the outcome is a Sprint Backlog to validate the Sprint Goal. When a plan is created for them, with their individual names allocated to a Product Backlog item before the event is even over, is it any wonder that the Developers immediately silo themselves and begin working on 'their ticket'? Of course not. We firmly believe allocating work (at any point) to an individual is wrong. At no point does an individual ever own the outcome of a single Product Backlog item.

Inviting SMEs (Subject Matter Experts)

Self-management involves knowing when you should be handling something yourselves but also knowing when you need help. Asking for help is not a problem (it may be a sign of an impediment with cross-functionality, but that's a topic for another chapter). Inviting experts to the Sprint Planning event can be hugely positive when you're working on a new Product Goal or something the developers know little about. It will support the following:

Product Owner: Despite being expected to have the most information about a requirement, sometimes they can't know everything. Having a stakeholder present can eliminate the time lag between answering a Developer's question and getting an adequate response.

Developers: For specialist problems such as legal compliance, automation, marketing, and sales, or anything they have limited experience with, bringing along an external expert can guide implementation. The Developers still own the plan and the Increment's production, but they can dig deep when answering the 'How' question of Sprint Planning.

Scrum Master: When an SME is present, the facilitation can often be much more free-flowing when producing the Sprint Backlog. It is more human rather than transactional, using a project management tool. Be careful, though, as this is a double-edged sword—'Well, I would do it this way, not the way you're planning on doing it' is a very real possibility.

15-Minute Sprint Hypothesis

One of the many idiosyncrasies in organizations is Product Ownership, as discussed earlier in this chapter. They are too busy (or sadly, don't care enough) to fulfill their accountabilities, which causes zero-value optimization—it can be so frustrating. When a Product Owner turns up to Sprint Planning and says, "So, what do you think we should be working on?" without any ideas garnered from the stakeholders, it is soul-destroying to Developers. They could potentially waste the next Sprint's effort by plucking an idea from the sky. As a Scrum Master, coaching the Product Owner to generate a Sprint hypothesis can be challenging. Creating ideas that are safe to fail while in an environment that prizes speed and volume at all costs is not a natural thought process, which is why we recommend using the '15-minute Sprint Hypothesis canvas.' We've reproduced it below, but it's free to use and download online. As the entire document states:

"The purpose of this tool is to help Product Owners make Sprint Planning more purposeful and guided. It does this by scaffolding hypothesis creation to the point where you can take your idea to the rest of the Scrum Team. It intentionally does not go beyond this step."

Walking your Product Owner through this canvas before Sprint Planning will help to order their thoughts and provide input into the Sprint Goal creation. Remember, "Start with Why." Well, Sprint Planning starts with this exact question, and this canvas aims to help solve it.

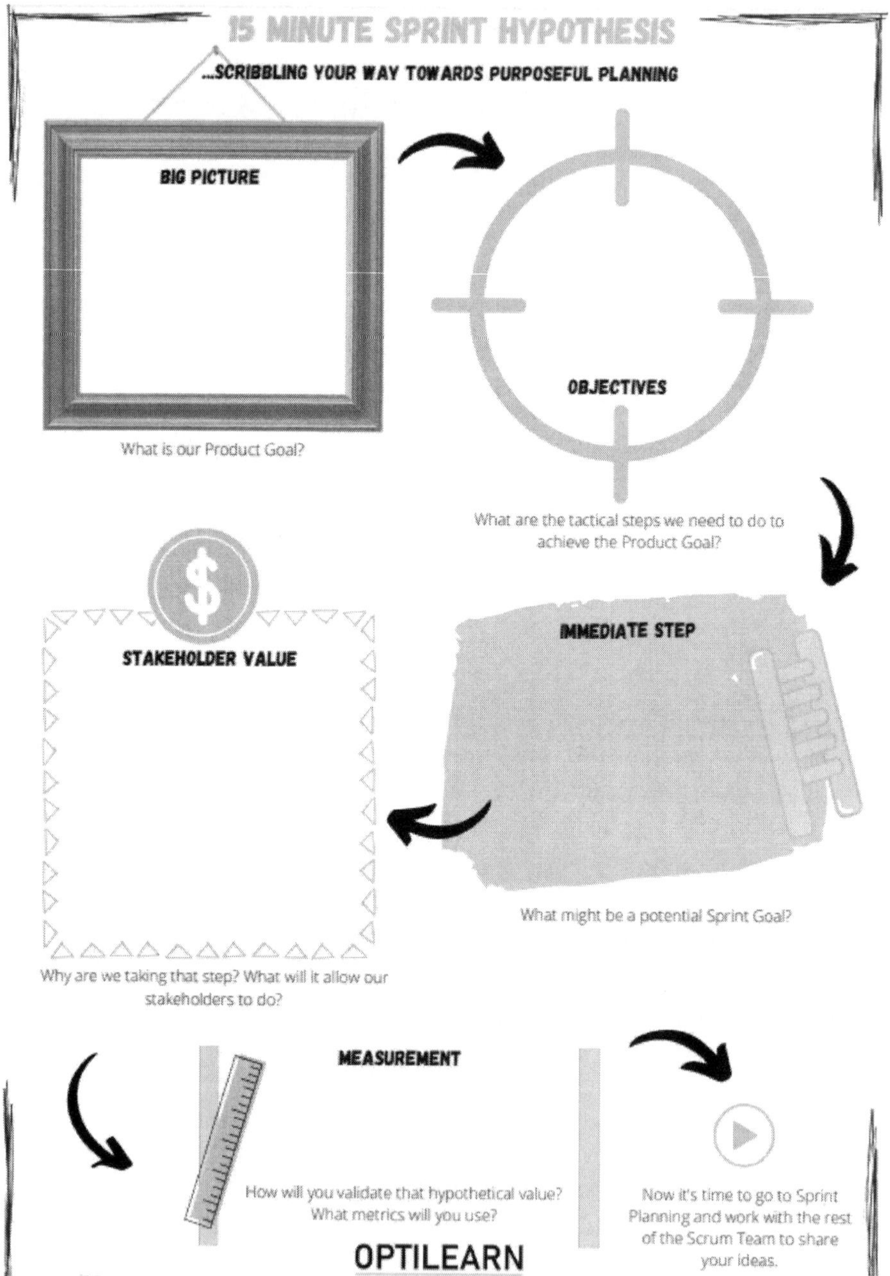

Figure 12 - The 15-Minute Sprint Hypothesis provides great input for the Sprint Planning.

Pyramid Planning

In our story, Roy couldn't pick one "thing" for the Developers to focus on. As Scrum practitioners, you have probably caught yourself saying, 'If everything is important, then nothing is important," and we agree. Everything has an order of preference (apart from your favorite child, although if we're honest, even that order does exist depending on the moment!). Without it, Sprint Planning becomes Sprint Planning**s**, because you aim to achieve multiple foci.

One of the techniques we've used to great success is Pyramid Planning. The idea is to start with the end in mind—the Sprint Goal.

A pyramid doesn't have two peaks; it has one, and all of the foundations we plan to build are directly focused on producing that peak. Putting the cherry on the cake is impossible without all the small pieces underneath it. One of the issues we often see in Sprint Planning is that the Sprint Backlog is already pre-populated with carry-over tasks, external requirements from other teams, and minor bug fixes. While Pyramid Planning doesn't preclude this work from being done, it reinforces that the work involved in producing the pyramid is where the value lies, not anything outside of it.

How can you use this? Stick your Sprint Goal at the top. That's the aim and a single focus. Anything dependent on your achievement of the Sprint Goal is added to the lowest level because these tasks must be done first (they are below the line because you may not be doing the work; external people may do them). They are the bedrock on which validation of your Sprint Goal will succeed. Without the bedrock, you are screwed. Product Backlog items that can be done once you have resolved dependencies are at the next level, with any bigger, more unrefined features being higher up. You start building from the bottom. The Pyramid shows that each PBI contributes to the broader picture.

It encourages buy-in from all Developers, even when working on something "tiny" because they can see why each PBI matters. Stakeholders love it because it's visual. You can color horizontals during the Daily Scrum to show progress or add/remove them as needed.

Sharing is Caring

We asked many Scrum Team members what their one tip for successful Sprint Planning is, and we've shared our favorites below. This section will appear throughout this book, and we are very proud. Firstly, it recognizes those awesome people out there working in the trenches, and secondly, it saves us from writing more sarcastic content. Everyone is a winner.

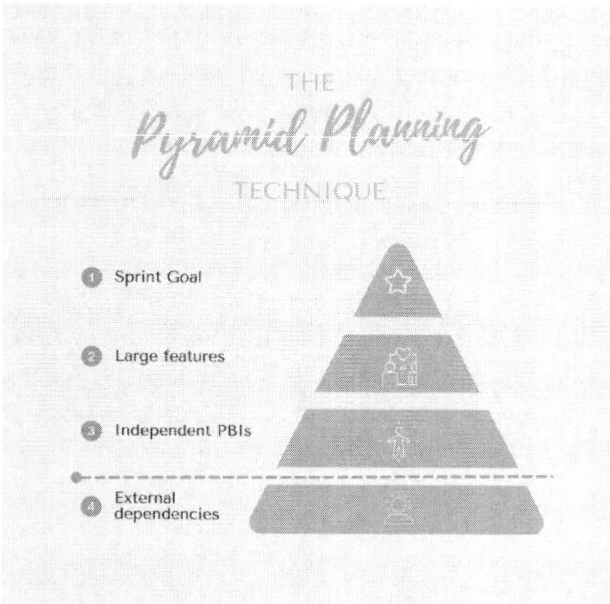

Figure 13 - A hierarchical approach that visualizes how each Product Backlog Item contribute towards an overarching Sprint Goal.

"Are you familiar with the song "The Skeleton Dance"? The knee bone is connected to the thigh bone... Try this at Sprint Planning. The Sprint Backlog is connected to the Sprint Goal; the Sprint Goal is connected to the Product Goal... I have found starting with the Product Goal helps Scrum Teams with focus when formulating their Sprint Goal. Perhaps a little sing-song can help as a reminder."

\- **Ryan Kent**

We often discuss the Sprint Goal as a tactical step toward the Product Goal. The Product Goal is vital to Scrum because it provides a target and focus. Ryan's great tip is to ensure we bring this commitment to the front of any planning discussion, such as the Sprint planning event. Without it, we may lose focus on the connection of this one small, tiny, insignificant Product Backlog item to the overall strategic vision for the product.

"Get into the routine of refining the stories before Sprint Planning. Ideally, refine the PBIs for Sprint N during Sprint N-1. Too often, I see teams try to refine during

Sprint Planning, which is exhausting, then the quality of the refinement drops during the event, and the team takes in PBIs with open issues that result in delays during the Sprint."

— Phil Comelio

Empiricism is always mentioned in relation to Scrum, and so it should be; it's awesome. But it often has a forgotten friend called "Lean Thinking." What we take from Phil's tip here is a practice usually found within Lean production called Kaizen. At its core, Kaizen means continual improvement, and this just-in-time approach that Phil is discussing is powerful. What's the point in refining halfway down your Product Backlog when the reality is that you're unlikely ever to go down that far? We'll tell you why; because it's easier to refine things in a future that is still calm and risk-free with unknown-unknowns. Compare that to the here and now, full of tactical dependencies, and you can see why. It's the same reason why managers will come back from a two-day offsite, having used company funds for food, drink, and a wonderful lake house (why are they always at a lake and never a Holiday Inn in the city center?) with a five-year plan—it's easier to plan the future than deal with "right now."

If we follow Kaizen, Phil's approach would have seen the Magnum Opus Scrum Team discuss improvements during their next Sprint Planning event. Do you think Roy would ever give them time to include that type of work?

Finally, and perhaps the most eloquent tip from someone who we'd describe as a product expert:

"Don't set yourself up for failure. Many times, I've seen teams pressured into forcing in so much work that the slightest crinkle causes everything to fall down—plan for success. Craft an achievable Sprint Goal and have a well-ordered Product Backlog so you can pull off additional tasks as/if/when they are achieved (if that is before the end of the Sprint). Everyone feels good when you "over-deliver." Very few, if any, feel good when the goal is missed."

— Gareth Amison

That last tip is a powerful way to end. "Don't set yourself up for failure." It's obvious when you think about it, but the problem is we never do. We ask for the team's capacity to be filled to 100% (because otherwise it's wasted utilization... right?), then when things don't go as smoothly as expected or a critical bug occurs, we wonder why we missed the Sprint Goal. Again. And again. If you've never seen the "Stress Bucket,"[20] we encourage you to look at the image below. Even though this idea is based on mental health, we could easily translate it into complex work in a Scrum. Swap poor diet and lack of sleep for unreliable infrastructure or corporate training. Rather than aiming for maximum output, which rarely equates to maximum value, how about aiming for a sustainable pace (or sustainable peace)? Part of this means treating the Sprint Backlog as a forecast to meet a single Sprint Goal vs. an executable list of items to be completed by the Developers. As practitioners, we need to work with our Scrum Teams so that they understand that the taps are never going to stop flowing. That "Oh, we'll do that when we have a quiet Sprint" mentality is a fallacy—it will never happen. If we accept the premise that the work doesn't stop coming, we can stop thinking about the taps or even the water. Our job is merely to make more holes in the bottom.

Figure 14 - Roy filling up the Stress Bucket.

[20] *Reproduced here from naturesaid.co.uk*

Ryan and Sander's Summary Feed (RSS Feed)

If there are any points that we want you to take away from this chapter, they are as follows:

- Management's focus on frequent updates regarding output instead of outcome can be detrimental. It's essential to prioritize delivering value over merely completing tasks.
- Efficient Sprint Planning relies on effective Product Backlog management and transparency. The lack of information and preparation can lead to rapid and ineffective planning sessions.
- Implementing metrics to determine which product areas are frequently used and understanding how users interact with the product can provide invaluable insights and guide development efforts
- Scrum Teams should self-manage, relying on transparency, inspection, and adaptation. Encouraging behavior-oriented phrasing and an "if this, then that" approach can enhance transparency and facilitate better decision-making.
- The Scrum Master should not be providing updates on behalf of the developers. Instead, they should facilitate self-management and ensure the team collaborates effectively without hierarchy.
- Work should not be allocated to developers by the Product Owner or Scrum Master. Instead, developers should collaboratively create the Sprint Backlog, fostering teamwork and shared ownership.
- Continuous Product Backlog refinement is crucial for maintaining transparency and ensuring that backlog items are well-understood and valuable. Techniques like split-team refinement and inviting SMEs can support this process.

Reflection

Use this page to reflect on the initial questions at the beginning of this chapter and what you may have uncovered throughout.

How does the lack of a clear product roadmap and outcome-based metrics impact the effectiveness of Sprint Planning in your own experience?

In what ways have you observed or participated in Scrum events where management's demand for frequent updates hindered the team's focus on delivering value?

How have transparency and communication (or the lack thereof) within your Scrum Team influenced the quality of the work delivered?

4.

Daily Recalibrating for Value

"You cannot make progress without making decisions."

– Jim Rohn

Preflective Questions

Daily inspection is needed to stay aligned as a team, prevent opportunities from slipping away, and avoid exposing ourselves to more risk. Doing this daily requires a certain level of discipline that not every team organization is aware of or even thinks about. Skipping one daily check-in lowers the threshold to do it again. Before you know it, inspection rarely occurs anymore, and we have let ourselves become zombies rather than highly skilled, knowledgeable workers who make the best decisions. Let's see where you are at.

What are the biggest anti-patterns you observe in Daily Scrums?

What would the impact be if daily inspections and discussions were held every other day in your team?

What immediate steps can you take to improve the situation starting tomorrow without needing additional help or resources?

It's been two months since the initial Sprint Planning event. Unsurprisingly, the Developers didn't deliver much value to their customers because they weren't working toward a common goal—their only focus was the sticky note that Roy presented to each of them. As time has passed, the developers and Jax, the Scrum Master, have become increasingly dejected by Roy's approach to product ownership. However, the upcoming Sprint might present an opportunity... because Roy is on holiday.

Before he left, he didn't provide any guidance on the most important work. "Take a look at the Product Backlog if you want some ideas," he said candidly as he swiped a bunch of sticky notes into the nearest trash can.

"Value maximizer, my ar*e" was one Developer's response to Roy's approach.

Annoying as this lack of direction was, it means that the Developers can spend time collaborating on a single Sprint Goal. Jax facilitates a fantastic Sprint Planning event that fosters a shared understanding—he uses a participative style to ensure everyone can contribute. Ultimately, the Scrum Team all agree that they have selected the most important next step to validate, so the Sprint begins. The Sprint Goal they choose is phrased as a question to investigate: *"Will the security gate hand scanner work for people of different racial backgrounds?"*

Halfway through the Sprint, things start to go wrong. The Daily Scrums have become transactional, with each Developer talking about what they have done and plan to do—there's very limited collaboration and even less focus on the Sprint Goal.

Jax starts. "So, what progress have we made toward the Sprint Goal, everyone?" He needed to say something, because yesterday they all stood there in silence waiting for someone to talk. It was really painful to watch, and there was no way he was letting that happen again. He decides to facilitate the event because, after all, without him pointing out whose turn it is to speak, these grown adults wouldn't be able to hold a conversation.

"I can't really remember what I was doing yesterday, but I'll probably carry on with it today," Johanna says with a chuckle.

"I was working with the legal team to decide at what age people can start to use our scanner. We all agreed that users must be over the age of eighteen," says Madhuri.

"Hang on a minute, I didn't think that was included in the scope of this Sprint, Madhuri? Weren't we just focusing on the technical side?"

The room falls silent because nobody knows the answer. There's clearly a misunderstanding here. The Sprint Goal isn't as transparent as they had thought.

To break the silence, Mackenzie adds, "Well, I got a little bit bored yesterday, to be honest, so I decided to pick up something cool from the Product Backlog." The rest of the Developers to stand there in silence. As they continue to rotate around the circle, Laurens chimed in.

"We just can't achieve this Sprint Goal. Everything we try and do is impacted by the bad decisions we've made over the past few months!" he exclaims, clearly annoyed and frustrated.

"Tell me about it. We've been focusing so much on delivering new features that we've not spent any time on delivering a stable product," says Alexii. "But I wonder if we've really told Roy just how bad it is?"

After a healthy discussion, Jax offers to help the Developers with how they can make technical debt transparent in the Product Backlog (this is the first impediment they've raised in months, so he really wants to remove it for them). They feel that as much as they enjoy moaning about Roy's failings, they probably could have been more transparent with the corners they have cut.

"Roy won't like it, though," jokes Jax. He knows that Roy had just started using Jira to make his Product Backlog transparent (because he wanted a way to share his ideas with the stakeholders). Jax knows that adding anything to it that shows the product wasn't perfect will definitely annoy him. "At the end of the day, though, Roy isn't here, and so we need to fulfil his accountability. I still wonder if we shouldn't wait for him to get back first to let him decide what to do?"

"Aren't you always telling us that we should make impediments transparent?" says Alexii. "Well, we want to do it."

After much discussion, the team decides that after the Daily Scrum, they will all meet to ensure the Product Backlog reflects the true state of the product. They know Roy won't like it, but they feel it's something they need to do. In fact, they even seemed enthusiastic to start dealing with the problem.

As the Daily Scrum progresses, the Developers continued to feel the pain of poor technical choices over the past few months. Everyone is just focused on their own work, and apart from commenting that they hoped Roy would slip and fall into the pool, there's no dynamic conversation between them, offering support to one another. It's obvious that their technique of answering *"What did I do yesterday?", "What will I do today?" and "Have I got any blockers?"* were not working for them. As each Developer spoke, the others weren't even listening – likely focused on 'getting back to work' as soon as possible. With Laurens' announcement that the Sprint Goal was unachievable, all the energy seemed to have left the team.

Just then, Sabrina walked past.

"Hi, everyone!" she said. "I'm glad that I've caught you all together. A customer has just asked for an important new feature to be added. I've told them that I'll pass the requirement on to you because Roy isn't in for two weeks. I've told them you'll have it done in about a week. They seemed really happy with that timeline." But as soon as Jax tries to ask a question, he's met with a swift answer before finishing his sentence.

"Can't stop; I've got another meeting!" Sabrina says as she walks off in a hurry.

"Quality. Looks like we've found our new "Roy," everyone." says one of the Developers.

The Daily Scrum ended. They all walked away, giggling at the joke but feeling destroyed inside. They felt unable to say no to Sabrina. They decided to skip adding the technical debt to their Product Backlog and instead jump on Sabrina's new requirement. After all, they only had a week to do it.

"Same ol' sh*t, just another day." muttered Jax.

<u>*Where do we go from here?*</u>

The Daily Scrum, affectionately known as the Daily Stand-Up by people who are... wrong, is crucial to the success of Scrum. It is a short, time-boxed event of fifteen minutes that brings the Developers together to synchronize their work and plan for the day. While it may seem like a simple routine, the Daily Scrum holds significant importance in facilitating effective communication, collaboration, and progress within the team. For these reasons, an ineffective Daily Scrum is not just an impediment to achieving the Sprint Goal but can be detrimental to delivering customer value. The story above highlights the potential of how this event can accelerate a product when done correctly, but sadly, it wasn't used effectively. Did they do anything right? Well, what is "right"? Many of us have experienced the realities of Scrum, and nothing is ever perfect. The commitment toward continual improvement pays dividends, and there indeed were moments in this Daily Scrum where this was apparent.

First and foremost, the Daily Scrum promotes transparency and communication within the Scrum Team. Even though it is an event by and for the Developers, that doesn't exclude the Product Owner and Scrum Master from attending as observers. Gathering together for a quick, focused event creates a platform for sharing updates, progress, and challenges. The "platform" referenced here is important—it doesn't follow the formula of yesterday, today, or impediments. In fact, if you've ever attended a Daily Scrum facilitated like this, we'd imagine you'd prefer being at the dentist. There is no rule that every Developer must speak, nor what can and can't be discussed. "By and for," the Developers mean just that; it's their choice how they use this event to maximize their chances of achieving the Sprint Goal. The Daily Scrum is a platform for frequent empiricism. This open sharing of information helps developers understand each other's work, dependencies, and potential bottlenecks, leading to better collaboration and problem-solving.

If you had to boil the purpose of the Daily Scrum down into one simple idea, it would be to validate the Sprint Goal as effectively as possible. At Magnum Opus, you will notice that even though the Sprint Goal was formed collectively, there wasn't a shared understanding—and this was the first ball they dropped. Other problems were the unwillingness to work together, limited cross-functionality, and poor-quality communication, which made inspection and adaptation even more demanding, and the facilitation technique was used. We want to elaborate on all these balls (hah, "balls") and provide some context for the whys, whats, and hows.

The Road to Nowhere

Let's imagine two similar situations.

Scenario 1 – You are on the road and driving toward a destination, a children's party; you know it will be unbearably loud. You don't want to go, so you pick up some cash on the way (because it's something you need to do) and stop off at the post office. You eventually get to the party, and it's just as bad as you imagined.

Scenario 2 – You are on the road and driving toward... anywhere. You find some cool things to do while driving along and enjoy your day. On your way home, you notice something epic you wished you'd planned for. Annoyed that you missed it, you make your way home.

You've probably already noticed the allegory at play here, but let's clarify: these are both bad situations to be in. In one scenario, we have a clear goal but are unwilling to move toward it. In the other, there is no clear goal to aim for, leading to missed opportunities for value. Many Scrum Teams that we work with exhibit one of the following behaviors when it comes down to it:

- Starting a Sprint with minimal buy-in to the Sprint Goal. The Developers don't care if the Sprint Goal is met and will, therefore, collaborate less, adapt infrequently, and go with the flow—they act surprised at the end of the Sprint when the Sprint Goal isn't met.

OR

- Starting a Sprint with lots of separate things to do but no clear idea of what would be the most valuable. The Scrum Team hasn't considered their customers and consequently neglected spending time crafting a great Sprint Goal.

Both of these situations are common, and both are equally bad. As anybody with children will tell you that children's birthday parties suck, but so does spending a day hoping something great will happen. The simple fix is not so simple in reality—it all comes down to Sprint Goals. Scrum Teams who lack a cohesive, engaging, and valuable Sprint Goal will find that facilitating an effective Daily Scrum is impossible. With nothing to work on together and limited interest in the outcome, the event will naturally move to a status quo of a status update. Nobody wants to be there, and the value is negligible because, well, what are you adapting toward? Sprint Goals provide a valuable framework and context for the Daily Scrum because they align the Developers, focus their efforts, enable adaptation, enhance transparency, and foster motivation. By incorporating the Sprint Goal into the discussions during the Daily Scrum, there is a greater chance that the Developers' work becomes purposeful and aligned with the product's vision.

So, why did the team at Magnum Opus struggle to create a shared understanding of the Sprint Goal they chose? We could easily place the blame at Roy's feet, but perhaps, in this case, that's not fair. In his absence, should the Product Owner's accountabilities be performed by someone else in the Scrum Team, yet no one has picked them up? In our experience, the failure of the Daily Scrum is caused by a series of dominoes that are hard to see. A lack of understanding as to where the product is headed leads to:

- The developers lose interest and enthusiasm for working on the product, which leads to...
- "Let's get this Scrum event over as fast as possible!", which leads to...
- A poorly defined Sprint Goal with everyone sharing a different understanding of it, which leads to...
- An unclear Sprint Backlog, with disjointed Product Backlog Items thrown in there, culminating in...

The Daily Car Crash

To break the feeling of being on a "road to nowhere," you can try a few different techniques. Fundamentally, their success will be determined by the culture of your team and whether they are willing to improve.

Five-Whys: This technique helps you get to the root of a problem. It's simple – start with the question, "Why is this problem occurring?" Then you keep asking, "Why?" until you find the real answer that you are looking for. Typically, when you ask a team why something is happening, you will get a symptom of the problem (and treating symptoms isn't effective over the long term). That's not their fault; they often haven't had the chance to think about it. Once you've repeatedly asked "Why?" a few times, the idea is that you are closer to the true root of the problem that you can try to solve. In Magnum Opus' Daily Scrum, what would the real root cause of their ineffectiveness be?

Just-A-Minute: This is a British game played on the radio—we know, old school, but it can easily be applied here. The concept here is that we want to keep the Daily Scrum short and sweet. When a Developer talks, they must remain on-topic (so, avoid talking about their favorite coffee shop or what they had for breakfast) and avoid repetition—if they don't, the Developers can buzz them. This technique can be great to reinforce the purpose of a Daily Scrum, but don't use it too often; otherwise, we can imagine they'll throw the buzzer at you.

Prompt Question: Jax tried to use this one, but it fell flat. Often, the most awkward part of a Daily Scrum is the beginning because no one wants to talk first—even though they talk perfectly well outside of the event (maybe standing in a circle is scary?). Jax tried to start the flow by prompting a conversation about the Sprint Goal, which is exactly what the Daily Scrum is for. As a Scrum Master, we sometimes fall into a bad habit of facilitating this event, and therefore, just starting the ball rolling by asking a simple question might be an easy technique for the Developers to use themselves. If you start by talking about the Sprint Goal as the focus, the idea is that the focus is on the outcome rather than someone talking about their output: more collaboration and less individualism.

You don't have to pick one of these—mixing up the techniques used in a Daily Scrum brings several benefits that contribute to the overall effectiveness of the event and the Scrum Team's performance.

Preventing Routine and Complacency

When a team follows the same routine every day, people risk going through the motions without truly engaging. Just look at Johanna's response in our story—she couldn't even remember what she was doing (and what's worse, she didn't really care). Introducing variety breaks this pattern and keeps everyone more alert and engaged. This can help prevent the Daily Scrum from becoming a mundane task and instead transform it into a dynamic and valuable interaction to gain different perspectives and fresh ideas.

Promoting Collaboration and Learning

Varying the techniques used in the Daily Scrum promotes collaboration among team members. People are prompted to interact more, share insights, and offer assistance when the format changes. This collaborative atmosphere fosters a learning culture where the Scrum Team can learn from each other's experiences and expertise.

Enhancing Problem-Solving

Let's not forget why we meet daily—to inspect and adapt. In short, we're there to solve the *problem du jour* and ensure we progress toward our Sprint Goal. Different techniques may shed light on previously unnoticed issues or provide alternative approaches to challenges. We want to create an atmosphere where participants are encouraged to think outside the box, which can lead to more effective problem-solving and innovative solutions.

Tailoring to Team Dynamics

Teams evolve over time, changing their needs and dynamics. Think about how immediately a Scrum Team changes when someone new joins. This is an example of homeostasis for the scientists amongst you*, where a process moves to regulate* itself due to changes. By using a variety of techniques, you can adapt the Daily Scrum to suit the current state of the Developers better. Some techniques might work better during intense development phases, while others might be more suitable when you're focusing on optimization.

Incorporating a mix of techniques doesn't mean abandoning the core purpose of the Daily Scrum; rather, it enhances it by keeping the event fresh, engaging, and productive. It encourages the Developers to actively participate, collaborate, and approach challenges with renewed enthusiasm, ultimately contributing to improved teamwork and product outcomes.

Owning Your Sh*t

*"Education is the difference between knowing your sh*t and knowing you're sh*t."*

You may have heard this before, but many years of consulting efforts have taught us that in Scrum, we collectively own the sh*t (even if many Scrum Teams don't act this way). There's no "I" in "team" like there is no single owner of a Product Backlog item. Therefore, there's also no single owner of the effort to turn work into a usable increment. One of the biggest anti-patterns we see in Scrum Teams is when they allocate work to an individual because when that happens, we lose the collective accountability for that work being turned into a Done state. Without shared ownership of the work, your Daily Scrum will fail (as we saw with Magnum Opus), as everyone forgets that Scrum is a team sport. Instead, each person focuses on delivering their own work first. You see, it's not just about knowing your sh*t but truly understanding the art of collaboration.

Collaborating within the Scrum framework holds significant strategic value, driving multifaceted benefits that bolster outcomes and dynamics. A Scrum Team becomes deeply and broadly knowledgeable by using its members' diverse skill sets and perspectives. An analogy might be separate rivers, each with its own water vs. all their volume in a single reservoir. When you work more closely together, you model behavior and transfer learning. Considering the Magnum Opus Daily Scrum, what did they learn from one another? Where were the lightbulb moments? Collective ownership is developed when a team thinks and acts as one. Furthermore, disseminating knowledge and best practices within Daily Scrum accelerates learning through rapid iteration of ideas. This continuous exchange of insights uplifts individual capabilities and contributes to a more proficient and agile team. This agility is particularly crucial for adapting to dynamic landscapes, where the team's collective wisdom needs to recalibrate strategies and tactics in response to evolving circumstances.

Another benefit of collective accountability is ethos. A collaborative ethos minimizes the pitfalls of individual blame and facilitates a culture of mutual assistance. Ethos is like a snazzy bow tie, making you stand out as an exceptional Scrum Team. It's the secret sauce that turns your work into something fun. Why are we using the word ethos and not culture? Are you thinking that? Well, ethos refers to the values and guiding beliefs that shape a group's behavior, decisions, and actions. It's about the ethical and moral foundation that underlies how you interact with others. A positive ethos is often associated with credibility and trustworthiness. It's like the personality and reputation that people associate with you. On the other hand, culture is a broader concept that encompasses the shared norms and customs of your Scrum Team. Culture shapes the environment in which you operate and the social dynamics that guide your actions. While ethos pertains to ethical foundations, culture encompasses broader shared behaviors that define a group's identity and interaction patterns. Ethos can be seen as a part of culture, as it influences how individuals contribute to and fit within the larger cultural context. We're taking the time to explain this because influencing culture can seem impossible in large organizations, so focusing on ethos can be the first small step. To improve ethos, here are a few things you could try:

Peer-Driven Recognition: Implement a peer-driven recognition system where Scrum Team members can publicly acknowledge and appreciate their colleagues' contributions. This reinforces the idea that ownership is collectively valued and celebrated.

Accountability Pairing: Periodically, pair Developers with the Scrum Master or Product Owner. This provides fresh perspectives and insights, fostering a sense of empathy that never hurts anyone.

Visual Metaphors: Use visual metaphors like an "ownership tree" displayed in your work area. As the Scrum Team achieves goals or overcomes challenges, people can collaboratively add leaves or branches, symbolizing their joint efforts.

There are more, though, and we'd encourage you to examine ownership impact walls, storytelling sessions, Obeya, gamified accountability, and ownership pledges, as all of these can affect an ethos of shared accountability.

One client that I work with used to use Lego to improve team ethos. The Scrum Team could select a model to build, and the organization would buy it for them. When a goal was met, however big, you could gift pieces to each other as a "well done," which were then added to the Lego model. Everyone could then tie their independent contribution back into something larger.

Team Specialisms

You've heard all the names: Quality Assurance, Testers, Graphic Designers, Marketing Specialists, Legal Experts—but what do these people actually do? They develop work for the product; therefore, we call them... what? You know the answer. We call them Developers. If someone is doing work contributing to the increment, they are part of the Scrum Team and the Daily Scrum. If work is being completed, it is done as a collective, and people with the 'Developer' accountability are the ones to do that. Not only because they are accountable for committing to the Definition of Done and are gatekeepers of quality but also because they need to make their work transparent. To do that, they need to attend the Daily Scrum.

A concept we often forget regarding Scrum is that teams can be dynamic. Although a stable Scrum Team can better forecast, complete work, and live the Scrum Values, nothing prevents a Scrum Team from dynamically adding or re-allocating Developers. For example, imagine Magnum Opus was starting a new Product Goal to ensure one of their biometric scanners is legally compliant in the United States. It is perfectly reasonable that they may want to bring in an external specialist for support. Before we go any further, there is something that we want you to remember—the Developer accountability is cross-functional and self-managing. Can you do us a favor and re-read that last sentence, please? The Developer ***accountability*** is cross-functional—we didn't say that every single developer is cross-functional.

It's absolutely okay to have specialisms in Scrum; however, we need to consider that the focus is on the whole accountability for producing a usable increment. Specialists like the ones we mentioned at the start of this section are okay to join the Scrum Team. Still, you shouldn't forget that they become a Developer, i.e., equally accountable for achieving the Sprint Goal and meeting the quality criteria described in the Definition of Done. They shouldn't join the Scrum Team if they aren't willing to do that. If the Sprint Goal hasn't been met, they should be willing to stop what they are doing and support the rest of the Developers to meet their commitment. Are they going to be team players? Or are they going to be solely working from their individual requirements set? If it's the latter, then we've got a problem.

So, where do we go from here? Reality is more complex than simply saying everyone should be able to do everything. We need specialist skills, which is undoubtedly true, but we also need people willing to do any work type other than their expertise. Willing is the keyword here, not able. Nobody can do everything, but we want team members to be willing to try. Those who won't could be accused of having a 'not-my-specialism' syndrome. Think of it like this: a team player isn't someone who only carries their own baggage. A team player is someone who holds more than their share when they can, even if it's challenging for them. They work hard for the good of the team. This syndrome is a tough impediment to deal with because:

- Specialists may perceive their value and contribution primarily through the lens of their specialism. They might believe that working on tasks outside their expertise devalues their unique skills and diminishes their professional identity.
- In many organizations, structures and workflows are designed around specialisms, reinforcing a silo mentality. It creates physical (and psychological) barriers to cross-functional work, making it harder for specialists to engage in activities outside their primary domain.
- Systems of recognition and rewards often emphasize specialized achievements. This discourages specialists from engaging in broader teamwork activities that are less likely to be individually acknowledged or rewarded.

Addressing these challenges and the 'not my specialism' syndrome requires fostering a culture of collaboration, emphasizing the importance of interdisciplinary work, providing appropriate training and support, and recognizing and rewarding contributions beyond individual specialisms. Fundamentally, though, our experience shows that specialists either get it or don't. If they aren't willing to commit to a team mentality, our advice is to show them the door—fast.

Robotic Collaboration

"Yesterday, I did this. Today, I will do that. No blockers." Has there ever been a sentence that strikes to the core of your professional existence as much as that? After a short walk around many corporate offices, we're confident you'd see more robotic, process-driven behavior instead of humanistic, error-prone ones.

- Let's get this over with.
- It's that time again. Let's decide on our next Sprint Goal.
- Do we even *have* a Definition of Done?
- Why are we doing this again?
- I can't remember the last time I spoke to a stakeholder.

Figure 15 - The same routine over and over turns people into robots.

These are common symptoms of being driven by process instead of value. No matter how experienced we are at product delivery, people tend to forget that the way we do it, our so-called "Ways of Working," are just guidelines. To share a brief example, consider a small business that uses an external accounting service. Every Friday, the director hops on a call with their accountant to discuss the week's expenses, invoices, and relevant tax deadlines. The accountant offers advice on tax efficiency and legal, but many areas are context-specific on which the director has to make the final call. In this simple case, the accountant provides a framework—general guidelines that are good practice to help keep the business afloat. On the other hand, the director offers the reality and uses it to make the best decisions given the circumstances. This way, Scrum (or any framework) provides the boundaries and rules suggested as good practice, but we are left to apply the human context. All this goes to say that without a well-understood context, the value you can get from robotically following a process is limited.

If you were to ask anyone what Scrum is, we'd bet that most would say it's an empirical framework (or "that's a rugby thing, right?"). If we were to go further and offer other possible answers, you might hear "guidance for product delivery" or even "a way to do Agile properly." Anyone who gives any answer like this (seriously, use the question as part of an interview) is missing the point entirely. Can you see what each answer had in common? Have you figured it out yet? Let us tell you: they all discussed Scrum as a process—something to follow. And it's when you're behaving like a robot. Take a look at Magnum Opus' Daily Scrum; what were they really aiming to achieve by having it? If they were being honest, the answer would almost certainly have been "because we were told to."

If we revisit our earlier prompt about "what Scrum is," do you have a better answer than the ones we created? If not, allow us to share our own.

Scrum is a people-centered, heuristic set of guidelines that can be leveraged to increase product value.

Now, we know what you're probably thinking... heuristic? If you know what that word means, we apologize profusely. However, for a moment, let's pretend you don't. Something that is *heuristic* allows an individual (or team) to discover or learn something for themselves. If we take a more technical angle, it describes a process of trial and error where the rules are only loosely defined. To us, *heuristic* describes Scrum perfectly, but it doesn't describe how most of our clients use it. In those cases, a better word might be *militaristic*.

Chicken or Pig?

No, that's not supposed to be an offer of food on an airplane. It references the old story of being committed or involved, but more on that a little later. Commitments are a unique social instrument that signifies how seriously you take something—we commit to our life partners, children, colleagues, and ourselves. The level to which we care about these commitments varies depending on our mood, the effort required, and the individual we're making it to, but we shouldn't forget that a commitment is not something we should seek to break lightly. Some people make them frequently, and others rarely, but their frequency of use is primarily irrelevant—the success of achieving that commitment matters. Who makes a commitment? You do. We'll forgive you for shouting out, "No! The Scrum Guide says the whole Scrum Team commits to achieving the Sprint Goal!" and, sure, it does, but your participation in the process bought you a free ticket to the party whether you wanted to go or not. Commitment is personal, and don't let anyone tell you otherwise.

In 2008, Bhaskar Mazumdar made an exciting discovery. Socioeconomic status—how rich you are—correlates more closely with siblings than their weight or height. Take two brothers as an example: It is more likely that at age thirty, they will have similar levels of income than they will be of similar height or weight. Why? Because while their genetics are incredibly similar, their parents' socioeconomic status was identical. The purpose of bringing this up is not to touch upon the topic of social mobility (spoiler alert, no one is blaming people for being white, male, and educated) but rather to discuss the fact that the choices we are presented with are not random. If you are born rich, you are eight times more likely to be rich yourselves than those born into the bottom fifth of family incomes.[21] Why are we mentioning this? Well, because this simple, random act of luck of who we were born to makes all the difference in our professional lives. It impacts our personal characteristics and, by extension, our willingness to make commitments—even to the level of something as mundane as a Sprint Goal.

As we discussed earlier in this chapter, the sole purpose of the Daily Scrum is to enable the Sprint Goal to be met. The Sprint Goal, i.e., the commitment of the Sprint, is conceptually a team goal that takes precedence over everything else. However, different people commit differently based on their attitudes and behaviors. These behaviors are pre-determined because some people are

[21] *https://ifs.org.uk/publications/why-do-wealthy-parents-have-wealthy-children.*

chickens, and some are pigs. Credited initially to Ken Schwaber (in the context of Scrum), this business fable of a chicken and a pig wanting to open a restaurant is legendary.

Figure 16 - Involvement and dedication are vastly different.

Just looking at this comic strip makes us laugh and cry. Too often in our professional lives, we have been unwilling pigs, i.e., when management makes commitments on your behalf. Forced commitment is not actually a commitment at all; it's an order delivered with a carrot or a stick. The carrot vs. stick approach is a cost and energy-intensive approach to the actual desired outcome—commitment born of collaboration. When we work together to determine, progress, and deliver an outcome in which we all have a shared desire, it is cheaper and more likely, in our experience, to deliver on time, at cost, and a higher quality product.

As a call to action, consider your current work themes, both professional and personal. For each, write whether you are a chicken, a pig, or a passive observer. All three positions are acceptable but only if you accept the level of influence (or lack of) that comes with each. The funny thing about being a chicken, pig, or something else is that it really comes down to the level of autonomy we want regarding the solution. Suppose you're walking around a restaurant, and the waiter tells you where to sit, irrespective of whether that is where you would have picked had you been given the autonomy and empowerment to decide. In that case, you instinctively like that location less. Similarly with your products, feature development that enables customers to personalize it (e.g., the color scheme, landing page, data layout, notification type, etc.) gives them an unconscious stake in your product because you have given them the autonomy to choose. This works in all aspects of life—a personal choice will always trump a decision or commitment made for you.

Turning the Wheel Toward Value

The Daily Scrum is an opportunity to adapt toward value. However, this is only true when the developers understand where value truly lies. If you walked up to them today and said, "What do our customers want right now?" would they be able to give you anything more than a guess? If the Product Owner has done their job properly, the developers may collectively stand up, form a circle, and chant the Sprint Goal at you like Betty White and Sandra Bullock in *The Proposal*, but in our experience, this is unlikely. Instead, they will point at the lists of tasks they have been asked to complete within the next few weeks and say, "That." With that in mind, if no flexibility, creativity, and adaptation are possible, then there is no point in having a Daily Scrum because all you'll get is a status meeting, also known as the killer of all vibes.

Imagine you're waiting for a bus, and the timetable says, "Buses arrive approximately every thirty minutes." Is that a helpful piece of information to decide whether you're going to wait or walk? We've all been there (especially if you live in the European capital of crappy public transport—the UK), and you don't know whether you've just missed one or if one is around the corner. Transparent progress updates are vital to empirical decision-making, so even if the timetable had said, "A bus will be here in five minutes. Last updated: seventeen minutes ago," you'd be just as unable to decide as before. The London Underground understood this when they greatly improved user satisfaction in the late 1980s and early 1990s, but not in the way you'd expect. They did it not by making the trains faster or more comfortable but by simply adding dot matrixes to show when your next train would arrive.

Figure 17 - Lack of transparency creates a longer perceived waiting time.

This concept is called the Psychology of Waiting[22]—people are more willing to tolerate a longer wait for a table at a restaurant or on hold for a doctor's appointment if that wait has an element of certainty (if you want to geek out, look at phone call hold queue strategies). This is all relevant to the Daily Scrum, as one of its purposes is to enable rapid decision-making and improve team self-management. Well, if all you've got is each developer giving an unintelligible status update about an unclear piece of work, of course, you aren't going to get energetic engineers jumping to help each other swarming around a joint commitment. To solve this, you need to know what drives the team (emotionally) and then teach the Product Owner how to craft Sprint Goals that scratch that itch.

[22] Maister, David (1985): https://davidmaister.com/articles/the-psychology-of-waiting-lines/

Ryan and Sander's Summary Feed (RSS Feed)

If there are any points that we want you to take away from this chapter, they are as follows:

- The Daily Scrum is vital for team synchronization, communication, and progress toward the Sprint Goal. An ineffective Daily Scrum can hinder progress and reduce customer value.
- A daily opportunity for inspection can be a platform for Developers to validate the Sprint Goal and adapt their work. It should not rigidly follow the formula of yesterday-today-blockers but be used to maximize the chances of achieving the Sprint Goal.
- Techniques for Improvement:
    - Five-Whys: Identify root causes of issues by repeatedly asking "Why?" to dig deeper into problems.
    - Just-A-Minute: Keep discussions concise and on-topic to maintain focus and engagement.
    - Prompt Question: Begin with a question centered on the Sprint Goal to foster collaboration and focus on outcomes.
- Mixing up techniques in Daily Scrums prevents complacency, promotes collaboration, enhances problem-solving, and adapts to team dynamics.
- While specialists are important, they must be willing to contribute beyond their expertise and embrace a team mentality to avoid the "not-my-specialism" syndrome. If they can't, they don't belong in a productive team.
- Scrum is a heuristic framework, not a set of rules to be followed robotically.

Reflection

Use this page to reflect on the initial questions at the beginning of this chapter and what you may have uncovered throughout.

How effectively does your team use the Daily Scrum to validate collective progress toward the Sprint Goal?

How might your team's ethos and collaborative culture affect your Daily Scrum's success?

Reflect on how your team approaches specialization during the Sprint. Are there areas where 'not-my-specialism' is hindering collaboration? How can you encourage team members to be more willing to step outside their comfort zones to support each other?

5.

DATA-BASED ADAPTATION FOR VALUE

All the measurements in the world are useless if you don't make changes based on the data.

– Amber Naslund

Preflective Questions

"We want to improve our ability to do X." "Coding quality needs to go up by X percent." Great! We get that. Shockingly, when we ask about either's current state, we are often met with dead silence. How can we improve if we don't know where we start? We, as a human species, are about constant progress. We want to do better, do more, and do faster all the time. But if we don't take the time to create a starting point, how can we verify that we have achieved said goals?

What aspects are you currently measuring in your organization/team?

If nothing, what is stopping you from doing so?

How do you know whether the things you measured have improved satisfactorily?

"We've been running around in circles now for hours! We're getting nowhere. We've been having this same discussion over and over. I think I need to escalate this to my own higher management."

Roy, Johanna, and Madhuri are discussing some new wishes with stakeholders, but they can't agree on the details. Especially when it comes to delivery dates, the stakeholders need their new babies to be in their hands way before Johanna and Madhuri feel confident they can do it. Roy isn't even sure that they will actually benefit from delivering these specific features.

"We need to have a social media sharing button in our portal," claims Kendra, Content Marketer. "People constantly show off everything these days. Enabling our users to share they have passed through security instantly can send a signal on their travel progress to their friends and family."

"I get your perspective, but I'm ninety-nine percent sure this goes against the entire GDP..." Before Roy can finish his sentence, Richard—one of Kendra's minions' colleagues—interrupts him.

"Who cares about GDPR?! Laws are just guidelines. Targets to aim for. We'll deal with the backlash as it comes."

"It's not even your job to deal with these things! You clearly know nothing about laws and regulations, so don't start slinging false claims into the conversation when you know nothing about the subject." Johanna gets fed up with these seemingly involved people, who, in fact, have nothing to truly add when it comes to value for the product the team has been building for a while now.

Kendra closes her eyes and takes a deep breath. "All right... We think this feature will improve user satisfaction. And that's all we care about, right? So, let's implement this little, tiny button. It's literally just that; a button. How hard can it be?"

Roy decides to take the items into the Product Backlog but makes it clear that they will investigate whether this GDPR trap, yet not per se, built it. There's no guarantee. This ends the meeting with Kendra and her colleagues, to the relief of Roy and his teammates.

"Improve user satisfaction... What do they know about that? Or care for, for that matter..." Madhuri notes.

Roy gazes into the abyss for a second, seeming to find something in that abyss, and then comes back to life.

"Now you mention it, Madhuri... **We** don't even know what our user satisfaction is, either. How can we form compelling arguments about user satisfaction if we have nothing to substantiate that argument with? I mean, yes, we care about user satisfaction a lot. But we have no data on that whatsoever. We need to figure out how to measure our user satisfaction! Apparently, Kendra aims to increase that specific factor, but it's not really about the specifics of the social media sharing button."

"Does that mean... we have to talk... to our users?" Johanna and Madhuri ask in tandem, looking like they've seen a ghost.

A few days go by. Together with the team, they refine the concept of measuring user satisfaction. They decide to spend some time at the airports. Magnum Opus is selling their first scanners to people and interviewing them after they go through security. The responses they get are mixed. Eighty percent of people passing by want to avoid talking or are in a hurry. Some others who do want to talk include elderly people who just want to have a nice chat, some others who wnt to a rant about how the government will have all their data and use it to track their location, and a handful provide some valuable answers to take back to the team to work with.

The investigation includes two parts:

- **Overall satisfaction:** how the users are currently experiencing the way they go through the security process and how MO's scanners help or hinder them.
- **Missing elements or ideas:** The interviewees were asked what they would need to increase the satisfaction rate. The team also presented some ideas, in which they also asked the audience for input on Kendra's request.

The verdict: overall satisfaction is a 6.5 on a scale of 10. Travelers are content with how they interact with the scanners but still feel the security is a (necessary) ordeal. No ideas came from the crowd on improving the satisfaction or what they are missing apart from "making the process obsolete as much as possible." When presented with the idea of adding a social media button, only one out of thirty-two participants stated they would like that button to *"create new content for her job as an influencer."* Whatever that means. In fact, many were skeptical.

"People are already glued to their phones as is. The moment their items get through the x-ray machines and back to the rightful owner, the first thing they pick up is their phone. They're not concerned about their jackets and sh*t, it's that damned phone. It's already causing pileups now, let alone when they have to do their influencer thing when that sharing button is presented." Robbie King, security guard, could already see the scenario unfold if this feature were implemented.

Robbie's remark sparks an ominous thought with Jax when looking over the data back at MO HQ.

"Roy..." he asks. "Do you really know who our stakeholders are?"

Roy looks bewildered, as if Jax just asked the dumbest question in the world.

"Of course! Let me create a little list for you."

John
Kendra
Roy
Richard
Sabrina
Users
Airports
Vendors

Jax stares at the board. Raised eyebrows. Looks back at Roy. Back at the board. And one final time, back at Roy.

"Who are our users? Who are our vendors? Where does that guy Robbie fit in? Are all of the airports equal? Could there be more stakeholders than these eight you just listed? We're basing this company's future and multi-million dollar machines' success on **eight** stakeholders. And you, yourself, are one of them?"

Roy can see his point.

<u>*Where do we go from here?*</u>

Not every stakeholder is the same. Similarly, not every feature is the same. To make matters even more complicated, not every stakeholder interacts with the same feature in the same way. They might have different needs or problems they would like to meet or solve. So, now what? Let's start at the beginning. We must understand what to build if we want our product to be usable and used. The *what* is derived from the *who,* and we can also derive the *why* from the who. Rarely does product development start with the product in mind. The product is always secondary to the problem it is trying to fix. In highly innovative ideas, the why is the core of the development, after which the product can be sold. On the other hand, many product teams work with people who come to them for a solution. In that case, the development starts with *who.* This is just the start of the puzzle.

A student in one of our classes realized that he knew little about his actual stakeholders and had been serving either the loudest people or following the HiPPO (Highest-Paid Person's Opinion). He neglected all other forms of stakeholders. Realizing that this needed to change, he shouted, *"Stakeholder management is a freaking full-time job!"* It is indeed time-consuming, with the purpose in mind that we save time after understanding their needs. The better we understand for whom or why we are developing something, the more options we can discard.

In many organizations, we faced the same challenge. The product teams we worked with were separated by miles from their users and most impactful stakeholders. This disconnection leads to a misalignment of expectations and a higher risk of building the wrong thing. How can we expect those teams to create the solution for their users if they can't talk to them in the first place? They often rely on second, third, or sometimes even fourth-hand information. Many of us have done the Chinese whispers exercise in elementary school. The first person whispers a story to the next, the next player to the person standing next to them until the line is completed, and stories are compared in the end. Often, the original story has changed. Sometimes, information has been added or altered, and other times, information is forgotten. The same happens with our product teams, except the stories aren't compared to the original version. Disappointed stakeholders are on the horizon, yet the product teams take the blame.

We, the authors, are confident that you, our reader, can see why it's odd that we verify the original story in elementary school yet fail to do the same thing in business. We're being taught to do the work as fast as possible and to trust the person who is giving us the information. As much as we actively advocate building trust in the organization, we are still human. This scenario, again, is where we need to bring the people who create the solution to those for whom we are building it as close as possible.

We need those discovery and developmental processes. Additionally, verification is equally important. Lack of verification leads to Schrödinger's product: your product is in a quantum state. Until you inspect its state, it can be valuable, not valuable, or anything in between. Leaving out one of these elements creates gaps, which we visualize in the following diagram.

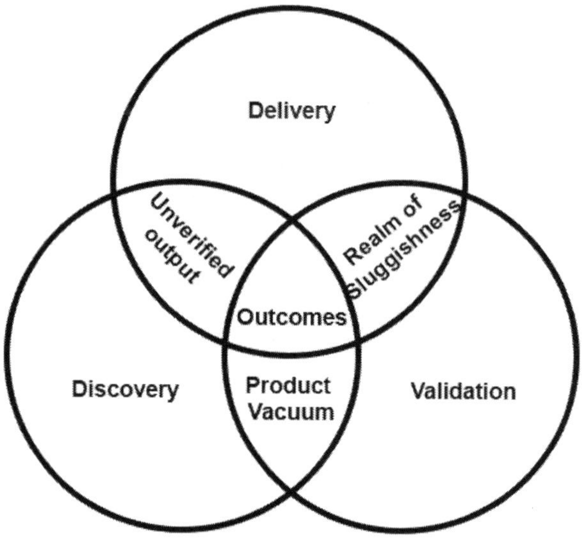

Figure 18 - The Value Creation diagram.

When we do our discovery work, we develop the product based on the results but never Validate whether we have built the right thing or our product is being used the way we expected; we have become a glorified feature factory. We're working with missing information.

If we develop our product without discovery but measure the results, the lead time will increase. When we go straight to the source to discover what to do instead of mindlessly building something, we find the right thing sooner.

Lastly, when we discover what to build and try to validate, we will soon learn that we skipped the step of making anything to validate. There's nothing there. We can't inspect something that doesn't exist. There's a product vacuum.

Therefore, we need all three of these elements continuously. These are not process steps, and this is not a waterfall-type process. They're constantly in motion and intertwined. Stakeholder engagement is at the foundation of success. Let's get that foundation in order.

Note: this chapter covers numerous templates that we have made available for free on our GitHub:

https://github.com/solving-for-value/sfv-book-resources/tree/create-mural-templates

Value Maximization through Proactive Collaboration

The Stakeholder Pyramid[23] is an excellent tool for supporting you and your organization with effective stakeholder management. It consists of five layers that cascade up, leading to Value Maximization through Proactive Collaboration. The top section is a result and goal for what happens in the lower areas. We'll start our inspection of the pyramid at the bottom.

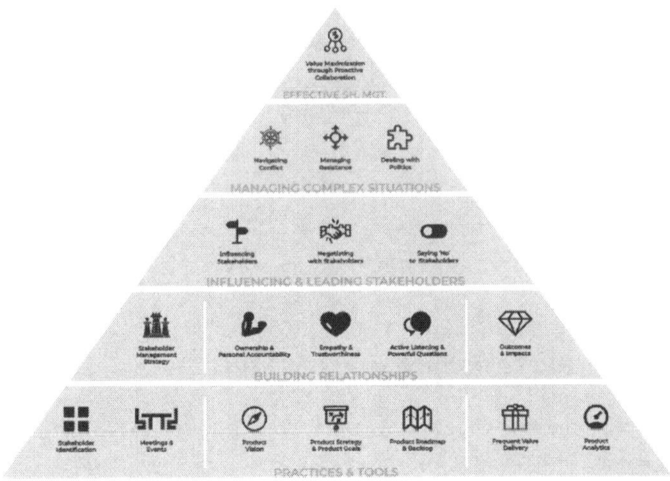

Figure 19 - The Stakeholder Pyramid by Robbin Schuurman and Willem Vermaak.

Practices & Tools

The most significant section of the pyramid contains the basic yet essential elements, starting with *Stakeholder Identification, Meetings, and Events,* moving

[23] *https://xebia.com/academy/nl/nl/whitepaper/de-stakeholder-piramide/*

on to *Product Vision, Product Strategy, Product Goals, Product Roadmap, and Backlog,* and ending with *Frequent Value Delivery* and *Product Analysis.* Understanding the impact specific stakeholders have or should have helps you navigate where to spend your time.

Even when you're not in a product management role or accountability, these elements are valuable to understanding what to build and why. We have seen many developers who were in hours of meetings with stakeholders who had low interest and low influence on the product, yet they pretended they had a lot with a dominant voice. It's easy to fall for these common traps that steer away from delivering impactful products, as we've been sucked into listening too much to the wrong people.

Building Relationships

We need our stakeholders, as they need us. There is an inherent reciprocity involved. When your stakeholders are involved and engaged in the whole process, you are armed with information to deliver to them. A healthy relationship is needed to understand the stakeholders' needs and build mutual empathy. This section of the Stakeholder Pyramid contains three blocks: *Stakeholder Management Strategy, Building Relationships,* and *Outcomes & Impact.* This section then supports understanding what your stakeholders are trying to do in their daily jobs and how you can help them achieve their goals. Who do they report to? What information do they need? What message are they trying to get across? Trying to see the world through their eyes is a powerful way to minimize your own bias.

Influencing & Leading Stakeholders

Many of us struggle with scenarios where it is hard to say no to others, where the entire scope has been fixed for delivery, or where hard deadlines exist. It is important to note the big difference between influencing and manipulating. The latter will result in finger-pointing and playing the blame game, while the former focuses on achieving the goals. These scenarios are often the hardest when the elements of the previously described steps are vague or missing. Again, we are working with lacking information, leading to wrong decisions. We are not saying that having these elements in place will magically make everything smooth and easy, but it definitely makes things eas*ier*. This section covers three elements: *Influencing Stakeholders, Negotiating with Stakeholders,* and *Saying "No" to Stakeholders.*

Managing Complex Situations

The second to last level of the pyramid discusses something many product managers or owners deal with power struggles, conflicts among different stakeholder groups, and resistance in many other areas. Conflicts are part of every relationship. Whether that's personal or professional, we are all different people, and we all have our own opinions. That's bound to clash somewhere. This doesn't have to be negative. In fact, many of the top-performing teams we've seen embraced conflict and made it something constructive. Keep the ownership to yourself as much as possible. We can't change someone else. We can only lead the way we would like it to be for others to follow. The same applies to resistance. Many people are reluctant to change. When we can provide a sense of continuity or understand their reluctance, it will be easier to deal with that resistance. This level discusses three last elements: *Navigating Conflict, Managing Resistance,* and *Dealing with Politics.*

As mentioned before, these levels cascade up. When the four levels mentioned above are embraced and dealt with, we'll be able to get to the top level. Unfortunately, this isn't like a video game where if we beat a level once, we are done with it forever. These elements must constantly be reassessed to ensure we do the right thing and keep track of changes.

Stakeholder Map

Digging deeper into the first step of the previous chapter, understanding where to spend our time with what (type of) stakeholder is essential. A practical tool for that is creating a stakeholder map. This mapping has many variations; we chose Mendelow's Power-Interest Grid.[24]

[24] *Mendelow, A. L. (1991) 'Environmental Scanning: The Impact of the Stakeholder Concept'. Proceedings From the Second International Conference on Information Systems 407-418. Cambridge, MA.*

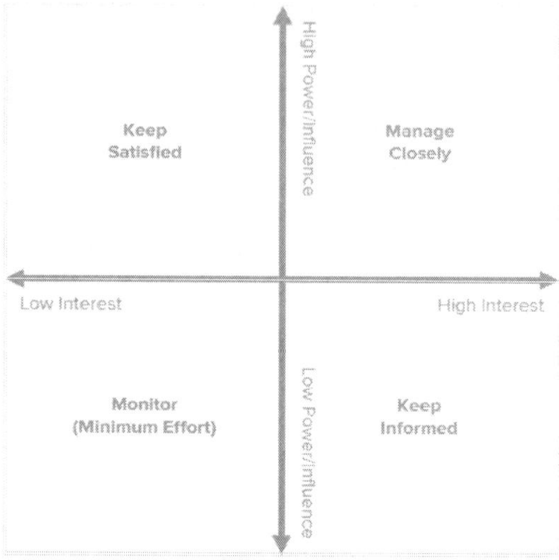

Figure 20 - Mendelow's Power-Interest Grid

This grid suggests to analyze our stakeholders based on two areas:

Power: To what degree can this stakeholder influence our organization or product?

Interest: To what degree is this stakeholder interested in the organization's or product's success?

Many stakeholders may seem to have much power and interest, but some have more than others. John, for instance, is highly influential in the organization and strongly interested in Magnum Opus's success. Governments that enforce GDPR compliance may have high power but little to no interest in Magnum Opus or its products. The relative position on this grid informs you to what degree you should engage with your stakeholders. It may even be interesting to discuss the position with a particular stakeholder to see if they would agree with where you placed them and if that should be different. Creating this grid collaboratively with your product team can result in beautiful discussions, deeper insights, and higher levels of engagement.

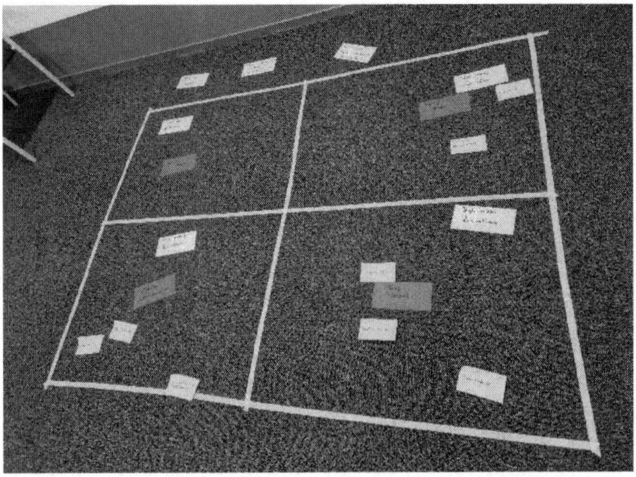

Figure 21 - Stakeholder Mapping in progress.

Stakeholder Mapping has several different forms. The one above is one of them. Others are, for instance,

- Stakeholder Radar
- Salience Model
- Stakeholder Relationship Model
- Ecosystem Mapping

Each has its own benefits and downsides. Choose the one that best suits your needs and style.

Stakeholder Management Strategy

Now that we know who they are, what should we do? Can we run off and start "informing" or "managing" our stakeholders? It's probably not the best idea yet. Do you know their preferred way of communication? Do you know what they need or want to achieve? If not, neither did Roy, so you're not alone. A Stakeholder Management Strategy helps you define this. The next page covers an example of Magnum Opus, available as a Mural template.

We highly encourage you to create one of these for your own context and validate it with the people you have listed. One of the biggest pitfalls our teams have experienced when creating these templates is working with sole assumptions and without verification. Dialogue creates deeper insights into your audience's views.

MAGNUM OPUS

Who (Name, Position, Team)	What (Information Needs)	Motivation (Real Goal/Problem)	Support (How to help)	Channel (How to Communicate)	Core Message (Contents)	Desired Effect (Stakeholder Group)	Key Influence (Who they listen to)
John (CEO)	Financial KPIs, Competitor Analysis, Opportunities, Risks, Vision, Strategy, and Roadmap	Ensure survival of the company	Collaborate closely on future plans and current strategy	Face-to-face meetings, reports, Product Wall updates	*"This direction is the one to ensure Magnum Opus become healthy again"*	Collaborate	Sabrina, Roy, Serge, Philipp
Sabrina (Project Manager)	Product Success indicators, Product Adoption Rates, Sales Numbers, Quality Indicators	Afraid of losing her job due to new ways of delivery	Collaborate in transition to new delivery ways, provide a sense of continuity	Face-to-Face, one-on-one meetings	*"With your help, we can deliver the best products together."*	Consult	John, Serge
Kendra (Content Marketer)	Numbers, Success Metrics, Customer Satisfaction, Employee Satisfaction, Quotes from customers	Want to create a high-value image to the outside world for Magnum Opus	Provide latest customer success and cool features	Co-creation through shared documents, face-to-face meetings	*"We are the best brand out there"*	Inform	Seemingly no one, she never listens

Figure 22 - Stakeholder Management Strategy.

By implementing a Stakeholder Management Strategy, we empower our stakeholders with the relevant information they need to excel in their roles, thereby significantly enhancing our product's success prospects. When combined with other tools such as Empathy Mapping, this strategy not only aids in navigating the political landscapes but also influences our stakeholders, aligning (organizational) goals.

Product Wall

The Product Wall, a powerful tool we will delve into, may initially seem overwhelming due to its wealth of information. However, it is designed to be flexible, allowing you to shape it to your needs. Its purpose is to tell a story and facilitate decision-making. What can we glean from this information? Do we spot any unexpected insights? What's our next move? Remember, this is not a rigid format but a suggestion that you can adapt to your unique circumstances. The Product Wall is available as a Mural template.

The problem, however, is that words like 'suggestion' are often overlooked or forgotten. Remember the 2017 version of the Scrum Guide? For instance, a snippet from the Daily Scrum that many of you who are using Scrum will recognize:

Here is an example of what might be used:

- *What did I do yesterday that helped the Development Team meet the Sprint Goal?*
- *What will I do today to help the Development Team meet the Sprint Goal?*
- *Do I see any impediment that prevents me or the Development Team from meeting the Sprint Goal?*

This first sentence is forgotten in ninety-five percent of the organizations we work with, and the event became dreadful to its attendees, as they would mindlessly go through the drill "because that is what we are supposed to do." Keep thinking critically.

"Authors, you're drifting onto tangents."

Ah, yes. Thanks! We like to talk. Or write. Coming back to the point, feel free to augment the Product Wall with the information that makes sense to you, your team, and your stakeholders. Metrics don't hold any value. It's how you decide to use the information and how your decisions are based on it that has the potential to deliver value. We included six areas:

- Roadmap
- Market & Domain Information
- Personas
- Models
- Value Metrics
- Customer Journey Map

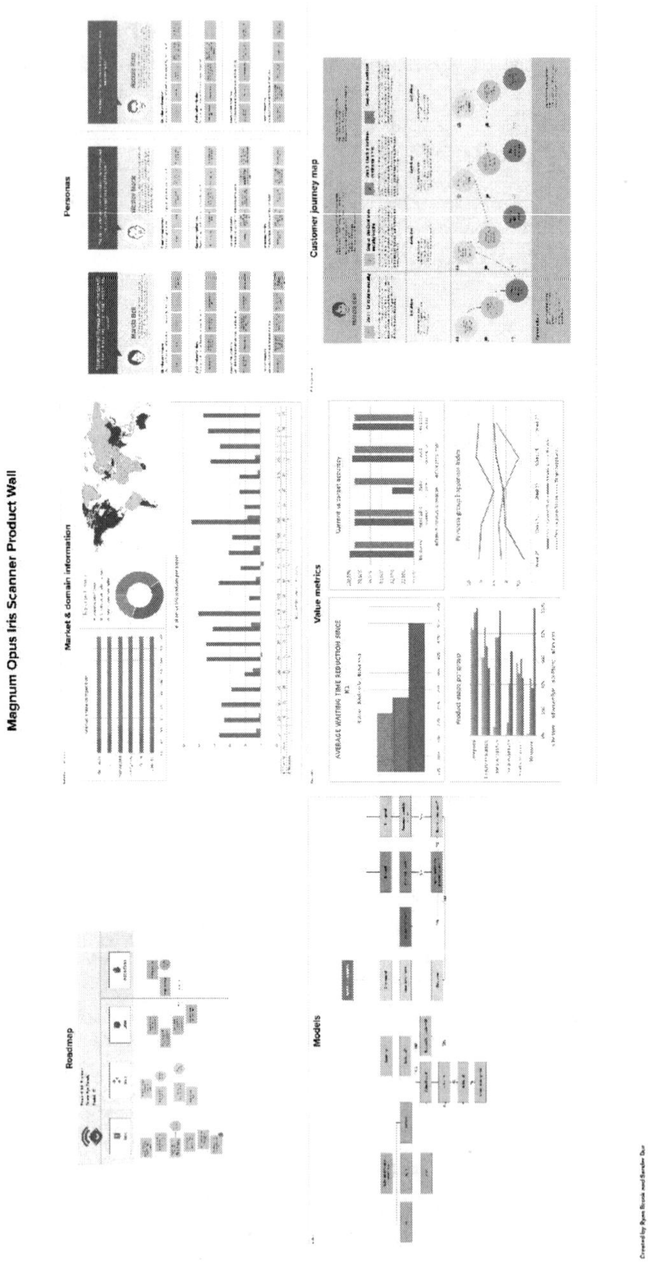

Figure 23 - This Product Wall is available as a free template.

Ideas to augment it could include:

- Product Vision
- Product Goals
- Product Backlog
- Budget
- Experiment Cards
- Release Schedules
- Quality Metrics

The power lies in the consolidated collection of elements that can help us recognize patterns and provide a general overview of the product's current state.

Roadmap

Let's define what a roadmap is and what it is *not.*

A roadmap is: a tool to create transparency around the product's vision, direction, progress, and order. It may change throughout the development lifecycle. It's a high-level, strategic plan for what is likely to be done in the future of development.

A roadmap is not: a fixed list of promises that teams must deliver during the following year, so management can base their budget on that and punish the team if they haven't met their roadmap. If that is what you are looking for, please close your laptop and never look at this book again.

Having clarified this, roadmaps can be an incredibly useful way of provoking discussion on what to do when, how they can affect releases, and what the order in the Product Backlog might be. Additionally, you may benefit from tailoring the type of roadmap to the different types of stakeholders you are talking to. There is not one single roadmap to serve all stakeholder groups. Think about the information they need and how you can serve that need. A few examples include:

- Now, Next, Later;
- Goal Oriented Product Roadmaps;
- Story Maps;
- Feature List Roadmaps;
- The Visual Product Roadmap.

For this example, we will use the "Now, Next, Later" option, as it is easy to use and easy on the eyes.

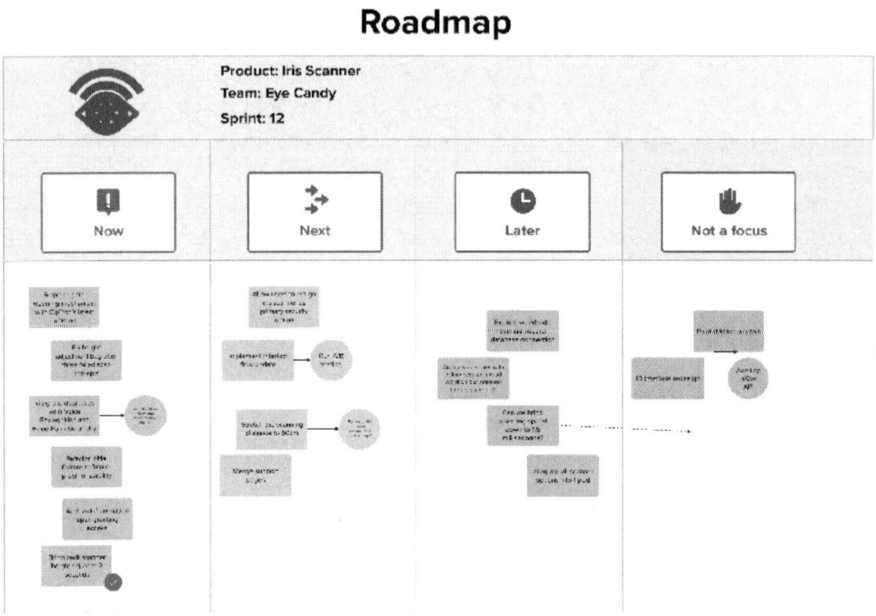

Figure 24 - A Now-Next-Later roadmap.

Let's break it down:

General product information: it lists what product is being developed, what team is working on it, and the number of the Sprint. Of course, this is just an example; you can augment it with whatever you like. Think of elements like date, updated version, link to stakeholder mapping, where to find the Product backlog, etc. It might be a good idea to refer to the Product Vision somewhere on the Product Wall so that everything on the Roadmap can be linked to achieving this vision.

Not a focus: For transparency, you can list ideas or concepts from stakeholders that are currently not critical enough to be developed or planned to reach Product Goals.

And, which may not be a surprise, the actual Now, Next, Later elements: What is our current focus? What are we likely to work on in the next one or two Sprints? And what may we be working on after that? There are certain Product Backlog Items in our example, with some high-level action items that can be things like dependencies or impediments that need to be taken care of (no, not by the Scrum Master per se.

Anyone can remove dependencies; the Scrum Master *causes* the removal of impediments but doesn't have to resolve them on their own). Note how these items contain ample details. This is done for a reason—to cause conversations with the relevant stakeholders. Y'know, Individuals and Interactions over Process and Tools. Something, something, Agile manifesto. Conversations are where potential value is discovered, and delivery and measuring validate our roadmaps' assumptions.

Like the Product Backlog itself, these items can be reshuffled. You can even add connection lines between items or color-code them to visualize their dependencies or relations.

Beyond Now, Next, Later

The Now, Next, Later roadmap might cover more on the Product Backlog. Or there may be some organizational requests to create (an arguably false sense of) certainty about what will be delivered in the coming eighteen months. Think about something along the lines of:

- H1 Business as Usual;
- H2 Sustaining Innovation;
- H3 Disruptive Innovation.

As consultants, we realize that theory and practice differ vastly. We appreciate the desire to know what will happen at the end of the year or beyond that. We would love to know ourselves, too. Do you know precisely what you will eat in the coming six months? We are confident you don't. Let's be honest: no one knows what the future holds, so making a budget based on probably incorrect arguments is nothing short of setting yourself up for disappointment.

We recommend experimenting with releasing funding based on outcomes created in the coming three Sprints or months. Did we achieve what we hoped we would? Then let's see what we can learn from that, look at our Roadmap, and see how much funding we need for the coming period. By adding this dimension to your Now, Next, Later Roadmap, the expected investments ahead are less of a surprise, and maybe even what the ROI has been, looking back. It makes specific discussions quite a bit easier.

Write with Pencil, Not in Stone

Again, we can't emphasize enough that those roadmaps, or Scrum artifacts in general, are not promises. They are forecasts that we can adapt based on new insights. Keep updating them as you progress and use them as input for decision-making. But keep thinking and talking; don't mindlessly follow whatever is planned at the beginning of the endeavor.

Market and Domain Information

If there is anything we would love to see more often, it would be active market and domain assessment by Product Owners. Product Owners are accountable for maximizing the value generated by the product the Scrum Team creates. Knowing where your product stands relative to the competition or how many of your products have been sold is essential for deciding the next steps. It can balance conundrums like "Can we build this product, and should we do it?"

Let's put that into a different perspective and take the streaming service market. There are currently over two hundred streaming services worldwide, some with a marginal difference from others, while some offer a specific niche like Formula 1, UFC, NFL, etc. These streaming services are available from any device, anywhere in the world. Now imagine that we start a new company to build an entirely new streaming service with an overlapping offer that competitors offer. As a unique selling point, we box our streaming service into a new TV. So, customers would need to buy our TV to use our service. A couple of questions would arise during investor meetings.

- Can we build the hardware? YES!
- Can we build the software? YES!
- Can we integrate both and build a solid product? YES!
- Would this product be sellable on a broad market? Highly unlikely.

Why, though? Just because we can doesn't mean that we should. Does this scenario *really* enable better service to our (potential) customers? Maybe some of them, but adding more features or locking in what the customers need in a device the vast majority already has creates waste. Data mapped in market and domain Information can help drive this conversation. Let's look at the Magnum Opus example.

These are just examples of all the other elements in our Product Wall. You can replace them with whatever you deem helpful. Remember that metrics by itself bear no value. Value is only an assumption until you deliver something into the hands of the user. We get to value by using data and metrics to base decisions on to lead the direction of the product. This example has four areas:

> **Market share relative to the competition:** Where do we stand regarding our competitors? Are we in a position where we want to be? What are they doing differently than we are that we could leverage? Or what can we think of to keep our strong position?
>
> **Top airport trends:** What are the current trending topics in airport security? This one is related to the case study we use in the book to illustrate development, but this could change to any product or organization. In this case, the trends are used to make a product fit the predicted needs of the airports Magnum Opus serves.
>
> **Geographical map:** Nothing else than a visualization of the areas where our products have been sold. If you plan to be the leading entity in Europe and your map shows Asia as the primary selling market, you might need to adapt your plans. Visualization is a compelling way to make specific things adamantly clear.
>
> **Number of active MO products per airport:** This could be translated to the number of products sold per region/area/whatever. In this, we look at our customers, how many of our products are in active use, and whether it's an increase or decrease. It immediately makes clear where most products are. This can link to geographical areas and other areas of the Product Wall.

Sprint Reviews are perfect events for discussing these elements with your stakeholders and team. Information radiators like the Market and Domain Information component support argumentation for certain decisions as a Product Owner, creating more trust and transparency between the stakeholders and Product Owner. Coming back to the funding discussion we discussed earlier, investors (a form of stakeholders, too) will be more likely to invest in your product and buy into the vision you set. For example, tools like this and the Roadmap can be used to determine potential work to move ahead of the competition and how much investment it would require.

None of this would matter if it weren't used to support the direction and creation of value itself. A short reminder that a product is defined in the Scrum Guide as "a vehicle to deliver value." So, all of these ideas, feedback, and concepts are directly put into the Product Backlog to create transparency and a shared understanding of the work that needs to be done. The next step is to link it to groups of stakeholders to figure out who needs what.

Personas

We need to understand our users to understand what we need to build. And much like creating a stakeholder map, there usually isn't just one type of user you serve. By creating fictional characters based on real user observations, developers understand how to design, build, and test the product and its increments to make it useful. Developers get a deeper insight into our users' needs, desires, experiences, and goals. Bear in mind that even personas are assumptions, too. They serve as input and inspiration for the product teams to form hypotheses that need to be validated later. Let's look at some example personas of Magnum Opus.

Personas

Figure 25 - Magnum Opus' personas.

Personas Are Not Individual People

To get that out of the way, a persona is not a highly detailed description of a person who has been interviewed once. It's more of a fusion of many elements in certain *groups* of people that use (parts) of your product. In this fictitious case, Magnum Opus creates biometric security devices airports use worldwide. We, the authors, frequently travel internationally, so we made observations along the way and talked to people to base these characters on. Besides that, you can have some fun with it, too.

I really struggled to figure out names for the personas for Magnum Opus. Then I figured I was making it too hard on myself. I used the names of three of my best friends (Robert, Wesley, and Mark), altered them a little bit because our user group does not only consist of men, and used an inside joke about fast food restaurants to finish up the last names.

Important to point out that these are made based on observations and not sucked out of thin air. Setting them in stone, much like all the other aspects of our Product Wall, would therefore not be recommended. It may lead to missed opportunities or false assumptions. Make sure to inspect and adapt regularly.

Our template is designed with simplicity and ease of use in mind. This approach allows you, our valued readers, to apply the knowledge you gain from this chapter swiftly. Let's go through the template's elements.

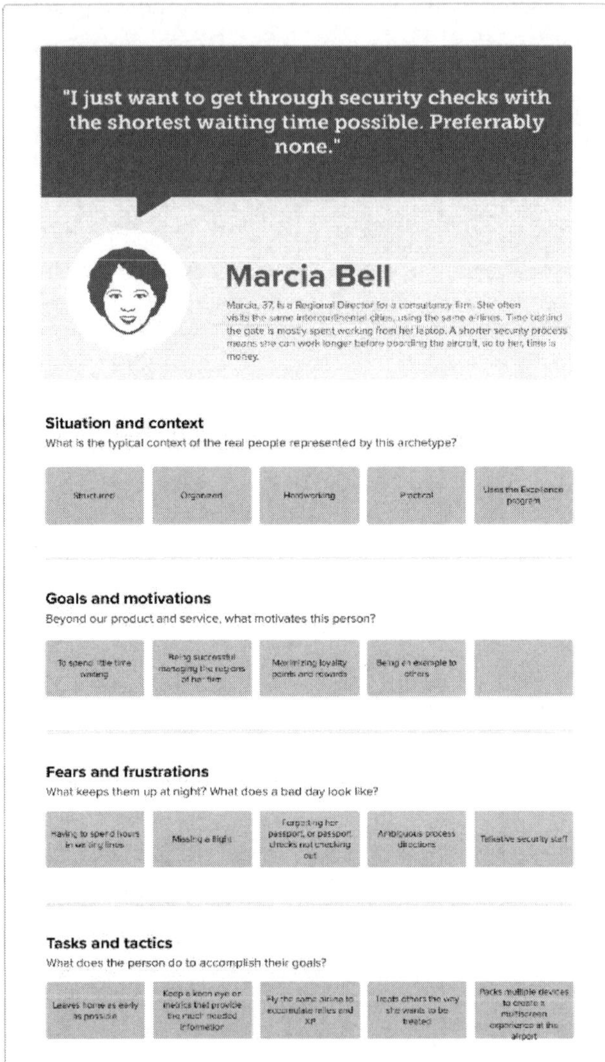

Figure 26 - Persona Marcia.

Personal goal or quote: Key to our understanding is the question: "What do these personas truly desire?" How would they articulate it? Grasping their goals informs our work and helps us identify unnecessary tasks. These goals could be directly tied to your product or the specific area or activity they use it for. In our example, we see a range of these. Marcia expresses frustration with the lengthy security process, while Wesley is more interested in the post-security experience**.**

Demographical information: Age, job, personal information, maybe some short additional information to put the quote into context. As mentioned later, you can add as many details as you want, but we decided to keep it brief and short. Knowing the demographic groups might provide information about their tech-savviness, for instance. Older generations might be unable to keep up with new technology, like Sander's seventy-four-year-old father.

Situation and context: In the template, we've chosen to stick to post-its to spark discussion and conversations. Putting in too much detail might make the developers biased or ignore other factors, as information gets handed to them pre-digested. "Situation and context" briefly describes some characteristics, traits, and what type of airport program she uses. The Excellence program unlocks premium perks like lounges, etc. This type of information helps to tailor the product to the personas. Put into a different context: people buying cars with a 5-star safety rating will highly likely not need a crash helmet. While cars like the Ferrari Monza SP1 and SP2 legally require a helmet to drive. Coming up with a prestige design helmet might be something that buyers of this model are interested in and willing to pay a premium price for, as the model can be displayed inside their homes as a demonstration.

Goals and motivations: What gets these people out of bed? What do they want to achieve? Are they excited to use our product? People like Marcia, frequent flyers, may find the airports a necessary evil. In contrast, Wesley is looking forward to being on-site, and Robbie is there every day to fulfill more of a transcendent purpose. How can you leverage these insights? What could Magnum Opus' clients (i.e., airports) learn from this? For instance, positioning certain security options at different places to optimize the experience for other groups, and so on.

Fears and frustrations: Knowing what keeps people up at night provides excellent input for the best experience possible. One of the things we noticed our Marcia persona does is get confused and frustrated when the direction or handling of a particular device is too ambiguous or takes longer than fifteen seconds to figure out. Looking at the UI/UX might provide a good move. These have a direct impact on your user satisfaction levels.

Tasks and tactics: What happens during "a day in the life of (insert persona here)"? How do they prepare for a trip, for instance? Are they heavily prepared, or are they fuzzy? Do they want to check in online a day prior? What options can we provide them with to take away as much hassle as possible at the airport itself?

Personalize Your Personas

Again, these are just a few elements. You can augment this template with whatever you need. Here are a few examples of what you could add to make it even more detailed:

- Pictures!
- Sliders to scale out certain areas;
- Data and statistics (for instance, how much time they ideally want to spend before, during, and after security);
- Channels of influence;
- Empathy maps.

We are not the bearer of truth (shocker, we know). We would *hate* to see people unquestioningly adopting this template and figuring it would solve all their Persona's issues. It does not. Continuous inspection and adaptation are required to keep this up-to-date and applicable. Users might change how they use and interpret the product over time, especially when added features are added.

Customer Journey Map

From the *Personas* onward, we can create *Customer Journey Maps* that illustrate how the user interacts with your product, as seen from the user's perspective. That flow starts prior to the physical interaction to create a scenario of what their day looks like. If we understand the scenario our users are in, we might be able to improve the product or help our users interact with it better.

We've continued to fill out the example with Persona Marcia in mind. A frequent business traveler who thinks the security process is necessary yet annoying. She wants to get behind security as soon as possible to work while waiting for her flight to take off. She opted to use the airport's Excellence Program, which enables her to use a designated, faster lane with state-of-the-art devices for a quicker process. Her "flow" of interacting with them is broken up into four stages:

- En route to security;
- Use Excellence Security booths;
- Check in for intercontinental flight;
- Find a work spot.

Understanding these steps helps us understand where she is, what she's doing, and what she needs at that stage. In return, this gives us more input on how we can improve the product.

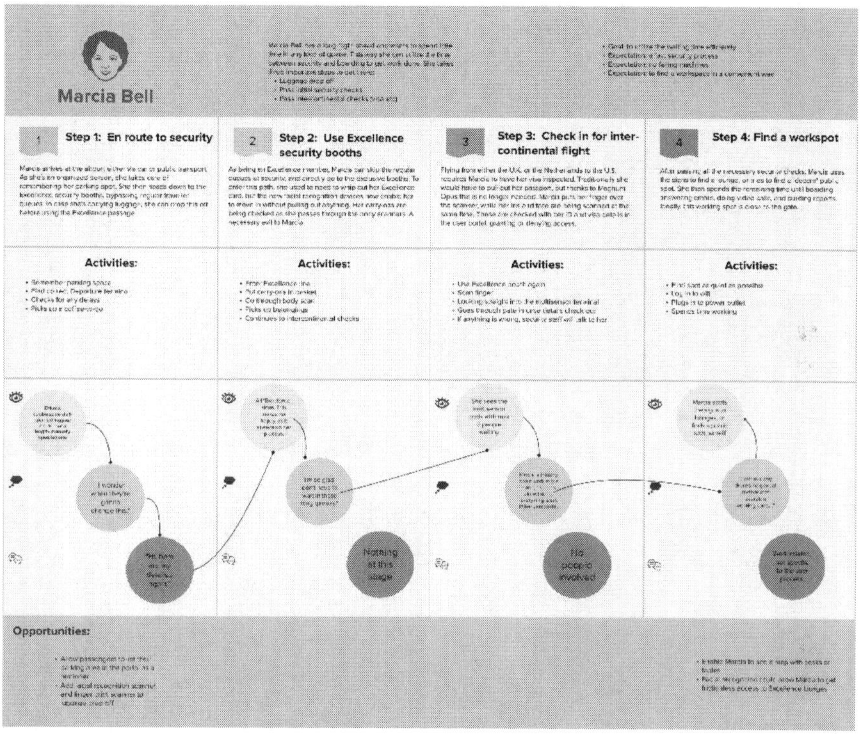

Figure 27 - Customer Journey Map for Persona Marcia.

The Activities show what you might assume: the activities this Personas is taking at that specific step. List them as specifically as possible. The second step in our Journey Map shows that's where Marcia interacts with MQ's machine for the first time.

The bubbles indicate what she sees, thinks, and says. The arrows indicate connections between those three and our product and the order in which they are used. When researching these personas, we noticed people who used something equivalent to the Excellence Program rolling their eyes when the regular booths were too busy and immediately continuing to the Excellence booths.

The level at the bottom of the example demonstrates opportunities. What are options we can think about to enhance our product? For instance, the fourth step shows she wants to find a working spot. Marcia, we found out in the *Personas* template, is someone who doesn't like hassle. She's very efficient. An opportunity here for Magnum Opus is to signal to the airport's system that Marcia has passed their security device so that the airport's app can offer Marcia a map with available working spots. We can leverage these opportunities to create experiments.

Remember that this and the *Personas* are generalized information based on observations. They are not hard truths. We cannot unquestioningly trust the info we listed in these templates and must keep evaluating to determine whether we have delivered the right thing.

Quality Metrics

Metrics provide valuable insights into your product's outcomes. They can show trends but also substantiate stakeholders' words. Data and words do not always match, which is input for conversation. Metrics can also show us whether we are delivering quality. In the example of this Product Wall, we listen to four metrics to inspect and discuss. Metrics by themselves don't hold any value. It's how we interpret and use them to potentially create value.

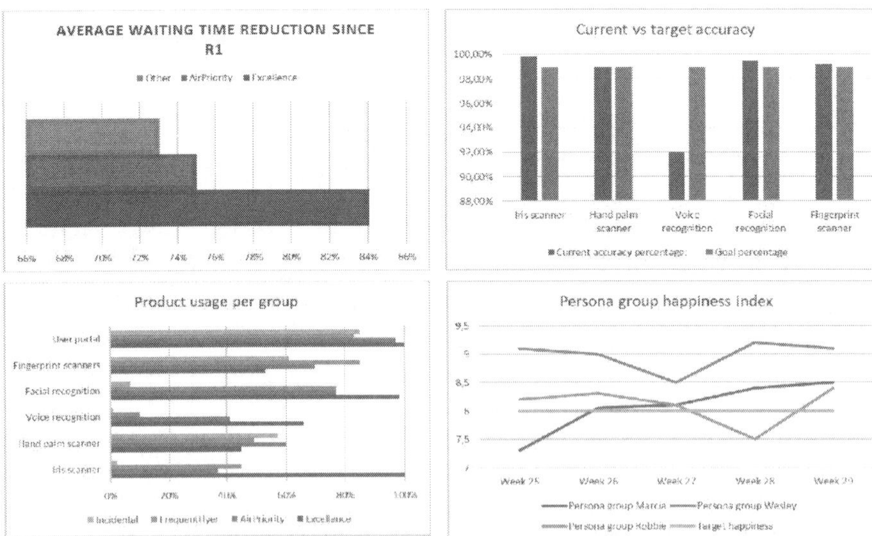

Figure 28 - Quality Metrics for the Magnum Opus products.

A team I worked with had very persistent stakeholders that insisted they needed a certain feature that they would use daily. Even though it did not align with our goals per se, our Product Owner decided to have it built, and the Developers tracked the feature usage. Over the course of six months, the feature got used once. Some good discussions were had after that insight was revealed.

What we can learn from the charts in this example is that the reduced waiting time after the product's first release is the most significant for the users of the Excellence program. Is that the right thing? We don't want to make it seem like we neglect AirPriority users or incidental travelers. Or maybe it *is* the right thing, based on the Product Usage statistics. After all, the Excellence users are the group with the highest usage levels.

"But what about Robbie?! He had a dip in his happiness."

Great observation! Indeed, he did have a dip, while Wesley's happiness went up. Should we do anything with that? Are they related? We can't tell based on this information, so we need to find out. It's all about the discussion and interpretation. This data is food for conversation.

Models

The models section provides a general overview of, for instance, the product flow or organizational composition. For example, this could be multiple teams working together in a scaled environment or reporting hierarchy. This is especially useful if we want to make the organizational impediments that may occur when they are addressed accordingly transparent. *Cough cough* Looking at you, Sabrina. *Cough cough*

This example shows the breakdown of the simplified iris scanner flow. When comparing these features with the roadmap, we can identify steps we need to add to make the international criminal database work.

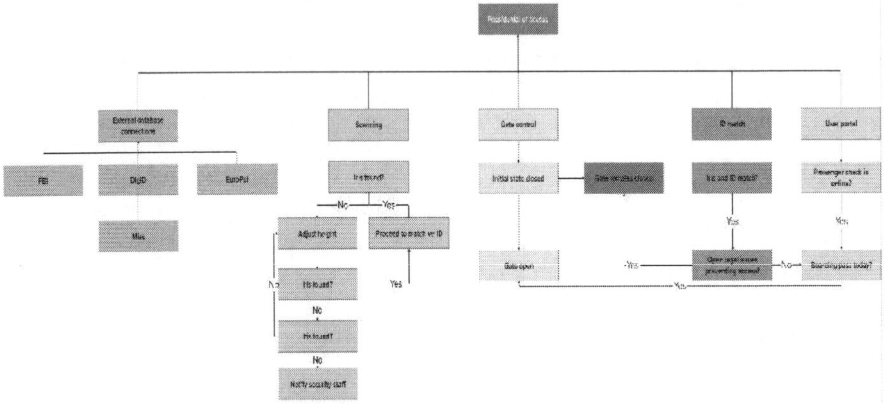

Figure 29 - Iris scanner flow model.

That discussion can provide information in return for considering whether it is worth the investment or potentially makes the product overly complex. There is already a EuroPol connection, and according to Roy, it could significantly support Robbie in his job as a security officer. Now, MO's developers can create a high-level estimate of how long it would take to develop. Then Roy can calculate the costs and risk and offset that against other features to decide whether it would be a good addition to an existing product.

Interviews

As stated at the beginning of this chapter, we will need to get our users to sit down with us to figure out what to build. Anyone can conduct an interview. Product Managers/Owners, Developers, etc. Anyone can. It is not exclusive to a role or title. As a product professional, the most helpful moment for you is to interview during or after the users interact with your product. However, we realize this is not always possible. Netflix's product managers are not knocking at our door after we binged *Brooklyn Nine-Nine* for the sixtieth time. A different form of surveying might be more effective in those cases. Equally, be prepared for the low agreement rate to participate in interviews. Don't get discouraged when many people decline your request. They're offering their time, and offering something in return might increase the chances that people are more inclined to participate in the interview. In the case of Magnum Opus, it could be something like a twenty-dollar gift card for the airport's duty-free stores.

Figure 30 - Developers talk to the users to explore their perspectives.

The Story Mining template is an excellent resource for channeling conversation and helping you remember what was said. At the center of the template is a picture of the interviewee. The old "a picture says more than a thousand words" still holds up. Ask them for consent to use one of their social media pictures or take a picture during the interview. Seeing the setting you were in during the interview makes it easier to relive the conversation and remember what was said. This concept will be important during the interview itself as well. We want to discuss the product and consider what we want from the conversation upfront. Now, we need to separate the *research* and *interview* types of questions. The difference is that the former is framed based on the goal, and the latter is derived from that goal to provoke answers that could inform our goal.

Here's an example:

Research question:

- *What makes travelers feel most safe and secure at airports?*

Interview questions could be:

- *What made you choose this specific airport?*
- *What alternatives were available?*
- *If any, what research did you do about security at this airport?*
- *Did anyone else tell you anything about the security process at X?*
- *What external influences were there in the decision-making process?*

- *Walk me through the day of commute—from the moment you leave the house until you arrive at your destination.*

Let the other person talk as much as possible. Give them time to think and recall the exact scenario and details. Remember, this is not a discussion; it's an interview to mine the interviewee's recollection. We are merely passengers in the ride portrayed by their synapses. It's worthwhile to ask open questions for clarification and detailing, but we challenge you to shut down your inner monologue. Take five minutes before the interview to ground yourself and make yourself aware of the fact that your inner monologue might pop up, and you can turn it off again. This allows you to focus on the interviewee with a higher degree. Powerful questions could include:

- Tell me more.
- What else (is there)?
- How did you feel in that moment?
- What did you notice made that possible?
- What leads you to believe that?
- What was the effect of X occurring/happening?

Avoid interrupting, but repeating the interviewee's last three words can help them feel heard and prevent misunderstanding. Reflect in timely moments to check whether you're both still aligned and then proceed. Do the same at the end. List a memorable quote from the interview that summarizes the essence of this interview. Thank them for their time and for how valuable their voice is to the product's success.

Figure 31 - The Story Mining template is also available for free download.

The Story Mining template provides four quadrants to structure interview input. It's available as a Mural template.

Scenario: What was the setting the interviewee was in? Who was with them? How did they feel? What were they doing?

As in the example: *"I wake up and get ready for the day. If I have to leave early in the morning, I pack my trolley the night before. If not, I first take a shower. That's not completely true. Sometimes, the airport lounge has a very decent shower, and I use that one. But most often, I take a shower before leaving. Artur is with me, so he constantly nags me to hurry up, although I know we always arrive everywhere in time anyway. We jump in the car and blast music. I love karaoke, so I repeatedly play Barbie Girl and sing along. We generally have a good vibe on these travel days. It's an adventure, and we get to meet up with good friends like Tom, Fred, and Antoni."*

Story: The summarized version of the interview story emphasizes key elements and research questions.

"My partner Artur and I were heading to our first conference together in a while. We're both public speakers and looking forward to being on stage again. Do you know what's funny about these security processes? Artur's ukelele always gets picked to run a search as if we can hide anything in there, ha!

Anyway, we're heading down from the parking lot to the gate. Obviously, we need to go through security. Annoyingly, the lounge is not conveniently located near security. I wish there would be a security option in the lounge itself. That way, our commute to the gate would be shortened as well. We often need to walk up to the end of the D terminal, which takes a good twenty minutes. We often take pictures in the lounge as a memory. We create these overviews at the end of the year of all trips we did together. That reminds me, it would be great if there were a way to have an overview of all the airports we've been to and when we went through what stage in the security process. Like Google Maps' history of your location.

When we head down to the gate, we try to make it as close to boarding time as possible. We hate standing in queues, so every minute we don't have to wait is brilliant. We do the same while in the air – we check the map of the landing airport so we know the shortest way out."

Exploration possibilities: These are purposely not called opportunities. Exploration of options is the step between general information and opportunities. We must analyze the story and scenario before formulating something that could provide opportunities for our company, product, or customers.

- *Discuss placement (of security machines)in lounges with airports.*
- *History in the user portal?*
- *How would that work with security and GDPA?*

- *Create an overview map with airports that use our machines.*
- *Can we provide information up front based on user, similar to personalized commercials, on where to go for the smoothest process?*

Insights: What did we learn from this interview that could verify or reject assumptions and hypotheses? What is something significant that stood out? Is there any overlap with other interviews we conducted?

The results of this interview and Story Mining support Product Discovery and are a foundation for crafting experiments.

- *Support Persona Marcia in short process time*
- *Experiment: create history overview*
- *Ukelele getting picked out*

Experiments

Great segue into the next chapter. Where would we be without experiments? Exactly nowhere.

"But aren't experiments risky?"

Maybe. It depends. But you know what else is potentially even riskier? Not experimenting. Not experimenting means we're relying solely on our experience. The problem is that past performance is not a guarantee for future success. Given the complexity and the rapid surge of new technologies, we *must* experiment. If we don't, someone else will do it for us, and we'll be eaten by those who do. That's ultimately the most significant risk. Besides that, we need to think about the problem we need to solve or the value we want to deliver. There isn't a straight path that leads us there. The puzzle of our product is like a maze; the challenges of product management and competition are like poker. Preserving options is essential, all while maintaining solid progress. Going all-in on a single option might be high risk and reward, but it rarely pays off. The problem we encounter continuously is people not liking the process of experimenting, as the outcomes may be uncertain. And we crave certainty.

Experiments enable the (contained) verification of assumptions to learn, rule out, or explore. We can leverage the outcomes of the experiments to define future adaptations of our product and our goals. Often, these experiments are phrased as a belief. In our Magnum Opus case, that could look like this:

- We believe that we can create a secure history overview of checkpoints of our machines.
- We believe we can partner up with AI company X to...
- We believe we reduce the number of criminals on the run by incorporating the criminal database connection.
- We believe our users feel safer if we build X feature.

These belief statements are high-level, similar to the research questions. We can then continue to break each statement into activities and tests to gather data to validate or reject the experiment.

- We will run twenty deep attacks.
- We will connect to EuroPol and FBI databases.
- We will run a test with five thousand travelers.
- We will interview fifty travelers in each segment (Excellence, AirPriority, regular) to collect interest numbers in feature X.

Many organizations leave it at this. But running experiments alone is not enough. What does this data tell us? Not a whole lot. As the diagram at the beginning of this chapter demonstrates, we need to validate, too. Not considering the quantitative numbers we want to learn from or when our experiment has been satisfied can diminish valuable opportunities and data transparency. That could be like these measurements:

- We will measure the number of successful attacks.
- We will measure the percentage of travelers interested in feature X.
- We will measure the number of people interested in upgrading their package.
- We will measure the number of inquiries after announcing the criminal record databases.

The last activity is to validate. When are we correct? When is our experiment successful? Taking the previous examples, that could look like this:

- The experiment is successful if there are zero successful attacks.
- The experiment is successful if thirty percent of interviewees are interested in upgrading.
- The experiment is successful if seventy-five percent of interviewees are interested in feature X.
- The experiment will be successful if we receive inquiries from at least twenty of the top 250 companies.

Figure 32 - Experimentation is essential for value discovery.

The experiment's results are valuable information for us to work with. Should we incorporate this into the Roadmap? How deeply is this related to innovation? (More on that in chapter 8.) How does the new information affect the current state of our product? This all is information for decision-making and taking the next steps in our mission of Solving for Value.

Setting Goals

Working with goals, or their absence, is a big challenge for many organizations. There are many different types of goals, so which ones should you work with? Often, frameworks provide their own set of goals. Scrum, for instance, provides the Sprint Goal, Product Goal, and Product Vision. Complementary practices can be applied to support the achievement of those goals. Many confuse goals, targets, and objectives interchangeably for the same purpose. Let's get that confusion out of the way first.

- **Goal:** Effect or outcome we want to achieve.
- **Target:** The degree to which we have achieved our objective.

- **Objective:** Actions or tasks needed to achieve the goal.

Short-term examples in the case of Magnum Opus' iris scan could include:

- **Goal:** Decrease the scanning time of the iris scanner by thirty percent.
- **Target**: Thirty percent or more.
- **Objective:** Remove redundant steps in the flow steps.

Now that we've gone through all these steps and gathered information, we're next in line to set some goals based on that information. We covered Sprint Goals in Chapter 3; let's look at some longer-term goals. Short-term goals are great, but we must not lose sight of the long-term objective, like the vision and overarching company goals.

Ryan and Sander's Summary Feed (RSS Feed)

If there are any points that we want you to take away from this chapter, they are as follows:

- Stakeholder relationships are not monodirectional. They are always reciprocal, some to a higher degree than others.
- We cannot sit and wait until stakeholders come to us with work to do. We need to be proactive and actively engage them in the development process.
- Product Walls are great tools for creating transparency for discussion and decision-making.
- Metrics alone don't yield any value. We need to interpret and analyze them for the decision-making process.
- Tools like Personas, Story Mining, Customer Journey Maps, etc. are great for creating user understanding.
- Experiments are needed in the uncertain environments of modern product development. Failing to experiment elevates risk.
- Setting and working toward goals creates focus and alignment.

Reflection

Use this page to reflect on the initial questions at the beginning of this chapter and what you may have uncovered throughout.

How often does your team engage with (prospect) users?

What is your current stakeholder management strategy?

What metrics are you using currently, and how do they support value delivery?

6.

REVIEWING PROGRESS FOR VALUE

Truth is confirmed by inspection and delay; falsehood by haste and uncertainty.

– Tacitus

Preflective Questions

Stakeholder alignment is necessary to ensure we are satisfying their needs. Building the right product is challenging without connection, understanding, or misalignment. As mentioned before, we make our progress transparent. But what use is that transparency if we are not talking to our stakeholders? Not engaging with the product's stakeholders leads to frustration, disappointment, and waste in the long run.

How often do your stakeholders attend your needed meetings to understand their needs and how the product satisfies them?

How many people in your team engage with stakeholders?

Is your team empowered to be proactive, or are you reactive to the stakeholders' voices?

Friday morning starts early in the Magnum Opus lab. Multiple demo pods with attached gazebos are displayed, standing tables with snacks are all around, Roy is standing in front of a beamer preparing his kick-off, and the energy in the room seems to be high. This Friday marks the end of another Sprint, closing off with a Sprint Review and Retrospective. Today, they have invited many influential stakeholders, and even some frequent flyers have agreed to check out what the team did.

Today feels different compared to previous Sprint Reviews. The team had a solid Sprint Goal ("Enable security gate pass by quick hand palm scan." They didn't make it, yet they still felt optimistic. The "quick" part proved to be the hurdle to overcome. Last weekend, Laurens accidentally deleted a large codebase when trying to install some changes he thought of. Overcome with enthusiasm, he made a terrible mistake that took a large chunk of the team's capacity to recover. Still, they learned a lot and collected valuable metrics that would provide a solid foundation for stakeholder conversations.

As the room filled with people, Roy knocked on his microphone to direct the attention to the projector and himself.

"Err, welcome everyone! Seeing so many people is a bit overwhelming, but it shows your engagement with our product. Thank you all for coming over! So, right, let's go over today's agenda."

After the past Sprint Reviews, Jax and Roy have been preparing the structure and content of the Sprint Review in-depth to increase the likelihood of a proper working session over a meeting with spongy stakeholders. As Jax said, "You know, like the where stakeholders just sit there like a sponge and wait for us to spill over all the information, and they just suck it up but don't really participate in our sessions."

"What are we doing here again?" Roy rhetorically asked his audience. "Let's go back to what we want to achieve over at Magnum Opus. Our company vision is to lead the way in transforming airport security through innovative and advanced biometric technologies. And everything we do in our team is there to advance toward that goal. Now, let's connect the dots. We don't get there overnight. We're not there yet. We create incremental steppingstones, deliver those, and inspect the best way forward. Between that dot on the horizon and right now is a strategic goal to make planning a bit less cumbersome and more realistic. The Product Goal we've been working on for the last month and will continue working toward for the few months to come states, 'deliver a handy security experience for all,' named after the hand palm scan we're creating. We have made another step toward that, as can be seen in this beautiful slide on our roadmap," he says as he pulls up a slide with almost unreadable details.

The speech was delivered so smoothly that Jax is unsure whether he should cry or throw up. Maybe a little bit of both.

"So, let's talk about the past Sprint. Madhuri will now take over the mic to do that. Give her a hand!" Applause arises as Madhuri walks up the stage.

"Welcome again, everyone, and thank you for your time joining us. To be direct, we didn't make our Sprint Goal. You see, one of our team members accidentally deleted an important part of the logic in the Increment, and it took us DAYS before we restored his mess."

Laurens feels his face become a tomato on steroids. He would have gladly just vanished into thin air at that moment.

"However," Madhuri confidently continued, "this gave us a harsh, but maybe much needed, eye-opener. We need to be more mindful of our fallback options and pay more attention to providing more stability to the product we have created so far. Don't get me wrong, we adore working with you on this product, but we have discovered that the way we have been working so far may not have been the best. Yes, we have created awesome results. Yes, we are a great team with inspiring stakeholders. But we can do better! More on that later in the *Metrics* part; for now, we would like you to experience what we have made this last Sprint."

Stakeholders need clarification about how they feel about Madhuri's words. Some look at each other, and some look excited to find out more.

"All right, as you can see over there..." she points toward the demo pods, "we have some actual working security gates lined up for you. What we did was create a hand palm scanner that is connected to the gate's opening mechanism. Upon first-ever check-in, a scan is made and connected to your profile. This allows the passengers not to have to pull out their passports, but just a mere scan of the hand palm is sufficient. This has also been checked with the existing face scan, and you are good to go. Or not, if you misbehaved in the past," she awkwardly chuckles.

"What we'll do today is demonstrate how this works, let you make a hand-palm scan and face scan for demo's sake, and measure the time it takes you to go through the entire security process. Bear in mind that due to us not achieving the Sprint Goal, LAURENS," she emphasizes his name to ensure everyone knows it wasn't she who deleted the logic in the Increment, "there is a lot more room to speed up the process between palm scan and the actual opening of the doors. We would like you to self-manage into equal-numbered groups and join one of the pods. Every pod will be served by one of our team members.

We hope you enjoy what we created, and we would love to hear what you think afterward."

Curiously, the fifty-six people stand up, look around, and attach themselves to people they already vaguely know or jump into unfamiliarity.

What ensues can be best described as organized chaos. Some pods suffer from the dreaded demo effect: everything had been running smoothly before, but it doesn't budge on moment supreme. Over at another pod, participants are so eager to test it that one person trips and falls against the connected laptop, causing a needed reboot. The others run smoothly.

"Let's join the other open security gates! Well done, guys! This is a great representation of the actual security process!" a frequent flyer jokingly comments. It alleviates some of the stress experienced by the Scrum Team members. In the end, the average pass-through time has been reduced by roughly twenty-five percent compared to the existing pods at the airport. Stakeholders seem delighted by this result.

When asked for feedback, Sabrina immediately replies, "Oh, right. That reminds me. I promised this other client of mine that you guys could deliver an update on their security cameras. They desperately need it. And as you guys do security stuff, I figured you could do this, too. I'll put it on the Backlog. I mean, you can do this, can't you?"

One developer, who had been silent until that point, shouts from the back of the room, "SUUUUUUURE... We *could* do that..."

"Great!" Sabrina replies, failing to hear the muffled, "But we won't, dumbest thing ever," that follows the developer's sentence. After collecting *actual,* generally constructive and positive feedback, Roy now goes on to the metrics part. He shows a few slides with lots of fuzzy details. Most metrics are quickly discussed without sufficient detail to make sense of them. A few stand out, however, and are adamantly clear. Stakeholder satisfaction is increasing; there are fewer defects, and the team's happiness is on a reasonable level, but also some less positive ones. Technical debt has accumulated over time and only displays an increasing line rather than a decreasing one.

Lena, director of a local airport security department, asks: "That line over there, shouldn't that be going down?"

The team members stare at each other, waiting for someone to speak up. Ultimately, Jax does.

"You are correct; that line should be going down. Ideally, however, in past Sprints, we have only been requested to deliver more features and not pay attention to the quality of the product itself. This has led to what we call technical debt, represented by this line here. Put into layman's terms, we're building this product on quicksand if we keep going like this."

Moments pass while stakeholders contemplate what was just said. "Can't we add a feature to make it better?" one stakeholder asks. The team members' faces answer his question.

"Let's do a little math here to feed the discussion." Jax continues as he writes it out.

# of team members: 9
Average internal rate: $55
Working days per Sprint: 10
Working hours per day: 8
Sprints needed to fix all TD: 6-8
Budget needed for TD clearing: $237,600 – $316,800

Some thuds could be overheard by jaws dropping to the floor.

"Just do it in 1 Sprint? It shouldn't be that complicated, should it?" a baffled stakeholder opts.

Jax stares at the stakeholder, trying to retain his composure before answering. "...It IS that complicated. This is the result of the decisions that we, as a collective, have made in the past."

"But Roy is the Product Owner. He should have told us about this before!"

Roy immediately jumps into defence mode. "You specifically told me to deliver the features because they were 'super important,'" he quotes between air-quotes.

"Alrighty, this isn't heading in the right direction," Jax interrupts the bickering. "Consequences of continuing to deliver more features and not addressing tech debt are decreasing our ability to innovate. Not innovating is what got us into a pickle in the past, so I think it's safe to say we all understand the dangers of that. On the other hand, if we jump on erasing all of it ASAP, it means that we can't work on any new work for a month or two. So, what do we do now? What makes the most sense? And where are we willing to invest?"

The entire group splits into smaller groups for a more organized discussion where everyone's voice is heard. A decision is made to address as much technical debt as possible in the coming Sprints and re-evaluate after each. Not everyone is happy with that, nor are they happy with technical debt in general.

Based on all the received feedback and decisions made, the Product Backlog has been reordered to reflect the technical debt on top. This shows everyone that new features are not the most important thing right now. This Sprint review feels good to the team. Not everything went well, and the Sprint Goal is still not achieved, but the stakeholders participated and shared their valuable insights. They made transparent decisions based on evidence-based management, and it wasn't a typical one-way event like the previous ones. This almost tasted like more...

Where do we go from here?

How do we know whether we are making progress? Would our stakeholders or users agree with what we've built? Is it as intuitive as we thought it would be? Regular get-togethers with our stakeholders are necessary to inspect the Increments created and validate our progress. In the Sprint Demo... (queue the recording scratching sound). "How dare you say the forbidden word?!" Right, right. The Sprint Review is the perfect time and place to align with your stakeholders. It is *not* a demo. Demonstrating the Increment turns your stakeholders into sponges. They'll be there physically and soak up everything you're showing, then leave the room only to forget what you showed them within a second. Just demonstrating the Increment limits the ability to collect feedback.

I worked with a team that told the stakeholders they made "the most intuitive UX ever." The developers clicked through the interface and showed all the features. Everything went smoothly. Until the users themselves started playing around with the demo environment, the Developers noticed many frowns and confusion galore. The users didn't have a clue how to interact with the new part of the product. We learned it was easy for the Developers because they knew how it worked, not because it was intuitive. We would never have found this out if the users didn't use the product while the

Essentially, engaging with stakeholders in these kinds of meetings builds a relationship.

A relationship works both ways. Stakeholders should bring the information the team needs to build the product and be available to support the team in what they need. The team should be working with respect for the needs of the stakeholders and the investment (money, time, and resources) to optimize the product to the best of their needs. And no, we still do not mean people as resources.

The scenario our team is facing in this chapter is not an anomaly. In fact, we reluctantly admit this is almost the de facto way we find eighty-five percent of our clients' Sprint Reviews or other similar events. Let's explore some improvement options.

Farmers' Markets

Farmers' Market Reviews are based on the concept of actual farmers markets, where local farmers sell their products directly to consumers. Often having booths or stands, the producers stand on one side of the booth, and the consumers on the other side directly interact with each other. The producers can tell specifically about the product's details, how it grows, the price, and everything the consumer needs to know. This works the same way with Product Teams and their stakeholders.

Create a setup with different developers pairing up to interact with stakeholders. They can share information about the product, the new Increment, metrics, etc. This enforces a relationship between stakeholders and the entire team, rather than the same person over and over. One of the biggest misconceptions we experience is that the Product Owner or Product Manager should "shield" the team from the stakeholders as if they are the devil.

Figure 33 - A great example of Sprint Review agenda.

Foster conversations and interactions between both sides. Let the target audience play around with the demo environment, and let the developers share information about the product, its challenges while developing, and additional information. This can rapidly expand the cross-pollination of information and mutual understanding, preventing the dreaded PowerPoint meetings. There are two acceptable reasons to use PowerPoint in the Sprint Review type of events:

- To *support* the inspection, not lead with it;
- You are part of the team building PowerPoint at Microsoft.

These Farmers' Market Reviews work amazingly in scaled environments, too. They can create a vibe similar to an actual farmers' market. We have even experienced situations where stakeholders started to "bargain" for features to be produced, which brings us to the following: Work Item Mapping.

Work Item Mapping

Our team is in a situation we've all been in before, and one of the reasons the need for business agility is so prevalent is dealing with emergent work. New insights, factors we didn't consider, or information lacking at the time of refinement constantly pop up. Dealing with that can be tricky. Stakeholders, like in the Magnum Opus example, value their work requests higher than others, and everything must have been done yesterday. Besides that, breaking up the work can lead to even smaller work items, resulting in a longer list of tasks to perform. Getting caught up in discussing what has priority and why it's not on top of the backlog is imminent. Then how should Roy deal with a situation like this?

Figure 34 - Stakeholder disagrees with a developer on where items should go.

Tools like Work Item Mapping can provide support in scenarios like the one above. Note: this book covers multiple maps and models. You should treat these like Leo di Caprio treats his models: pick the ones that fit your style best.

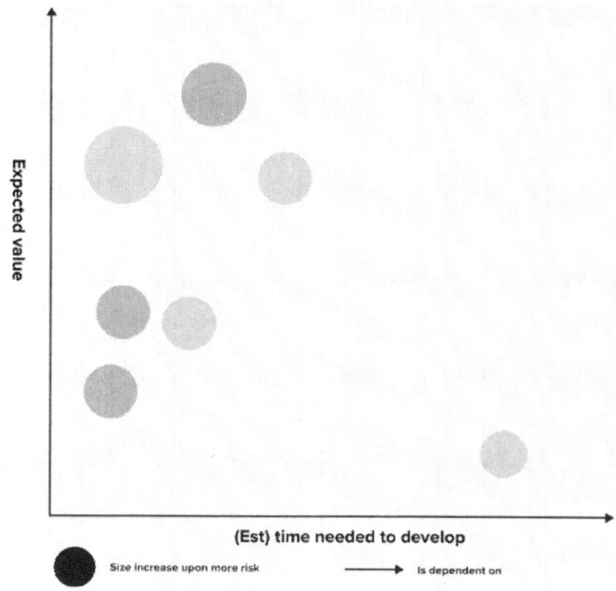

Figure 35 - Work Item Mapping step 1.

In this first step, we can see two features broken up into multiple pieces of work to get them done. They are color-coded based on the feature group. Delivering all the lighter elements creates feature A, and delivering the darker elements together creates feature B. Next, when these items are split up, they should be mapped accordingly on the Estimated Time to Develop (ETD) scale and Expected Value (EV).

"But, Ryan and Sander, why are you using such vague terms as Estimated and Expected? Isn't this map supposed to create certainty?"

The only certainty we can give you is that the outcome of this mapping tool, like any other map or model, does not grant you certainty due to the complexity of our work.

"Then why should we use it?!"

Excellent question! It creates transparency, drives conversation, and hopefully helps people understand why certain PBIs or other Work Items are ordered the way they are. It also helps Product Owners and Product Managers handle the challenging tasks of ordering that list.

Looking at this map at this point would make it easy to think we should order the top left ones first. Quoting legendary TV pitchman Ron Popeil:

But wait, there's more!

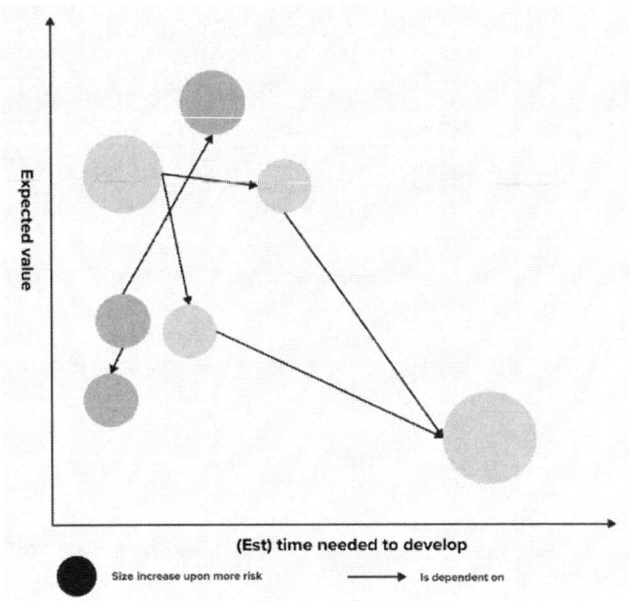

Figure 36 - Work Item Mapping step 2.

When we identify the dependencies of these items, it appears that the light, top-left item is dependent on two specific, smaller items that either have less EV or ETD. The same applies to them: both items rely on delivering the bottom-right item. This inherently means failing to deliver the bottom-right item will also fail all other light items. That is where size matters. The more risk the items bear, the bigger the size gets. Comparing this picture to the first picture, we can see the bottom-right item has now increased in size.

Because this specific one is essential to the development of the other three, the risk of *not* delivering it increases the necessity of timely, successful delivery. Other factors of risk include, but are not limited to:

- Missing out on competition;
- Receiving fines;
- Missing out on user expectations;
- Increasing technical debt;
- Longer time to verify or reject assumptions.

Like almost all aspects of product management, dealing with risk is a matter of choices. If the risk outweighs the reward, you might choose to take it. A great example of such risk paying out is when Drew Houston, CEO of Dropbox Inc., declined Steve Jobs' offer to acquire Dropbox into Apple (Business Insider, 2017). At the time, Dropbox had $116 million in revenue. At the time of writing now, in 2024, they increased to $2.52B and a valuation of $10B.

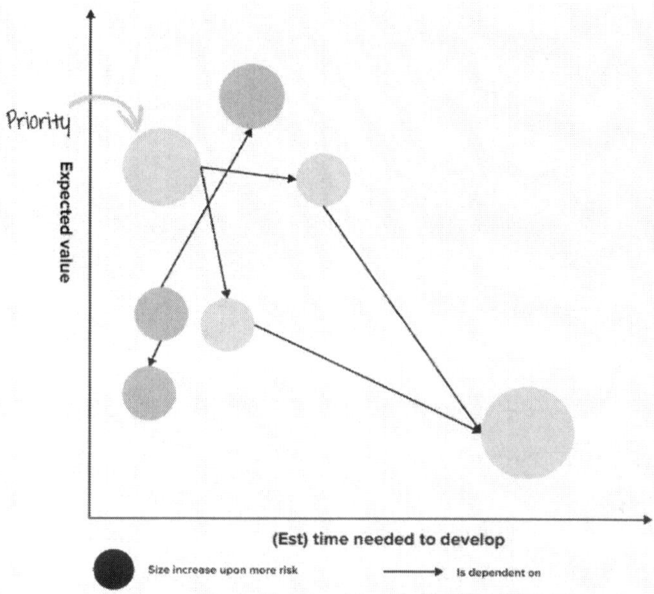

Figure 37 - Work Item Mapping step 3.

Sabrina told Roy she needed particular functionality delivered. Delivering the top left item makes that functionality possible. When asked, Sabrina says this item is the highest priority, making it the most important one for her. As many of you, our lovely readers, have probably experienced, what our stakeholders feel has the highest priority does not make this specific item the first on the list of development.

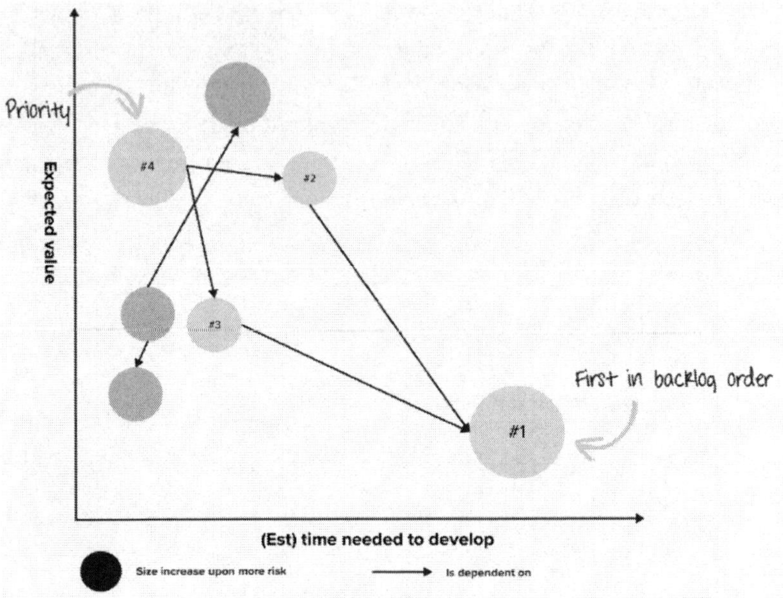

Figure 38 - Work Item Mapping step 4.

Due to the dependencies and increased risk, the bottom-right item will be at the top of the list, followed by the other items. Order and priority are two different things but are often mistaken for identical. Items can have the same priority, yet only a single order.

This mapping works for feature ordering. Then, it becomes crucial to know the goals beyond the short term. To find out more, go to our GitHub.

Ryan and Sander's Summary Feed (RSS Feed)

If there are any points that we want you to take away from this chapter, they are as follows:

- Inspecting progress without stakeholders is pointless. We must engage with them to ensure alignment and understanding of whether we are developing something valuable.
- Limiting ourselves to a demonstration of the Increment increases the risk of missing out on unspoken feedback. Remember that everything is an assumption until it is in the hands of the stakeholders. This event is the perfect moment to put the Increment in their hands.
- Different tools can support discussion and decision-making to increase the likelihood of building the right thing for our users.
- The Increment is only one part of the Sprint Review. Consider these elements:
    - Progress toward the Product Goal.
    - Metrics.
    - Budget.
    - The current state of the Product Backlog.
    - Figuring out what might be a good idea to work on next.
- Stakeholders are an *active* part of the Sprint Review. They are not there as an audience but as participants.

Reflection

Use this page to reflect on the initial questions at the beginning of this chapter and what you may have uncovered throughout.

How engaging are your Sprint Reviews or Product Reviews?

What do you expect from your stakeholders? And what do they expect from you?

What can be done to have more interactive and engaging Reviews?

7.

Introspecting for Value

"Improvement usually means doing something that we have never done before."

– Shigeo Shingo

Preflective Questions

Looking at your work is much easier when you know it went well. What matters, though, is being willing to look even when you know it didn't. Corporate environments are filled with practices ranging from completely stupid to surprisingly amazing, but whether good or bad, they persist without conscious change. Retrospection is a tool to unearth and identify actions you want to keep (and therefore continue) or prune (and stop).

How well do you use your Sprint Retrospectives to do this?

What is the role of a facilitator in a Sprint Retrospective? How does this align/differ from the Scrum Master accountability?

What are the three primary outcomes of an effective Sprint Retrospective?

How can you engage a Scrum Team with the concept of process improvement?

The Sprint Review has just ended. The Sprint Goal wasn't met, the demonstration turned into chaos, and the stakeholders left feeling confused. Overall, it wasn't an effective way to wrap up the Sprint. Everyone knows the Sprint Retrospective is happening after lunch, so the Scrum Team goes their separate ways to refuel. Roy tries to get a few people to accompany him to a new Portuguese burger joint called *Esquilo*, but everyone politely declines, as they'd heard bad stories about it.

As one p.m. rolls around, they all make their way to the meeting room, which everyone at Magnum Opus knows as "The Greenhouse"—four walls of glass accessed by one door in the middle of the office. It's the 'meeting room of last resort' because it's so hot and offers no privacy.

"Oh, man, it's the Sprint Retrospective again. Why do we keep doing these things every two weeks? Nothing ever changes!" says Johanna as she opens the door and steps inside. With a general nod of approval from the rest of the Scrum Team, she notices Laurens out the corner of her eye walking behind them. He looks angry. Unsure why this is, she shrugs it off and walks in to take a seat. Jax has clearly put effort into organizing the room before they arrived. Seats are arranged in small groups for teamwork, pens are available, and a nice welcome message is drawn on the whiteboard. As everyone settles in, he's about to start.

Suddenly, the CEO, John, walks into the room, looking exasperated.

"I'm glad I found you all. I need you to get back to work. Due to the mistakes made last Sprint, your release is late. Let's cancel this meeting and get back to it."

Everyone stays silent, but before long, they start to stand up to leave. The exasperation is visible, but without any form of empowerment, there's no chance that they'll object. After all, John is the CEO, and no one says "no" to the CEO...

"Actually, John, one of the things we'll likely discuss today is why this release was late. The purpose of a Sprint Retrospective, which is what this event is called, is to learn how we can improve our processes so that we're less likely to make mistakes in the future," responds Jax, with a slight weakness in his voice.

"Seriously?" John replies. "You and I need to have a little talk later, Jax." John walks away, muttering something about how this "bloody Scrum thing" is going to kill us and "what happened to the good old days?"

Just as Jax's heart rate begins to return to a normal level, Sabrina enters the room, pulls up a seat, and gestures to Jax to continue. Everyone looks confused.

"Don't mind me, I'll sit here silently. I'm only here to help," is her justification to all of the faces looking at her with incredulity. After dealing with John, it's a miracle that Jax can keep his cool. He calmly explains to Sabrina about the need for a Sprint Retrospective to create a safe space, and however much she wants to help, it'd be easier if she wasn't present. Jax is clearly on a roll today, thought the Scrum Team. As the door is closes behind her, he begins to hand out sticky notes to gather opinions as to the success of the previous Sprint. "I want you all to write down the worst thing that happened in this..." he started.

Then, without warning, Laurens stands up. He begins shouting and pointing his finger at Madhuri. "How dare you blame me in front of all our customers! In that Sprint Review, you made me look like a complete dick!"

The tension in the room is palpable. Everyone is waiting for Madhuri to speak. Clearly shocked and perhaps even a little bit scared, she finally responds to Laurens. Her response is measured but forceful.

"I'm sorry, but I was just telling the truth." Her tone clearly shows she's ready for an argument. "If you hadn't deleted the logic, we'd have met the Sprint Goal."

"No chance. Not with the crappy quality work you've been putting out recently," Laurens launches back at her.

Within seconds, Alexii is involved, then Roy, then Johanna, and eventually, the whole team picks a side. It's Laurens vs. Madhuri—a Magnum Opus "Royal Rumble." Before long, people are swearing, ignoring opinions, and are disrespectful. What they had all forgotten about, though, was that this meeting was taking place in a room made of glass—The Greenhouse. Everyone in the office could see what was going on. Unable to take their eyes off it, they're all keenly interested in what is happening. They can't hear anything, but the body language isn't good.

Jax stands there looking incredulous. This happened so fast that he realizes he's still holding his sticky notes, waiting to facilitate a purposeful Sprint Retrospective! It's clear that the time for encouraging a bit of active listening is over. This is a conflict he needs to resolve... and fast. As all good Scrum Masters will tell you, techniques start rushing through his head during a conflict. Empathy mapping? 5 Whys? Troika Consulting? *What can I use to help?* he thinks.

He's spurred into action when he hears Madhuri cross the line. "If you keep making mistakes like you did this Sprint, Laurens, I hope you get fired," she says. But as soon as she'd finished her sentence, she knows she's gone too far.

"Right, everyone!" Jax bellows above the noise. "This is getting ridiculous. I know we've just started, but we're going for a coffee break. Come back in ten minutes, please."

Everyone leaves the room to a sea of eyes staring at them from around the office. It's a walk of shame, and everyone feels it.

With ten minutes to get his head around what to do, Jax remains in "The Greenhouse." He could swear that every part of his body was sweating.

Right, he thinks to himself, *You've got this.* He's worried about the argument continuing during the break and the two sides becoming more entrenched in their opinions, but he has no control over what people think. All he knows is that he needs to get things back on track.

After ten minutes, everyone slowly starts to return. They aren't shouting anymore, which is a win in Jax's eyes. He tries to make light of what just happened.

"Let's start again. So, we need to find a resolution to this sh*tuation," he says with a small laugh. The joke doesn't land at all. The team may be calmer but still incredibly angry about what happened before. *Tough crowd,* thinks Jax.

Someone needed to break the silence. When Roy starts to speak, everyone turns to look at him. Without any negativity in his voice, he defends Laurens and encourages people to put themselves in his shoes.

"We've all made a mistake, right?"

Taking the opportunity with both hands, Jax breaks them into two groups to complete an Empathy Map—one team could focus on Laurens, and one could focus on Madhuri. This leaves Laurens and Madhuri free so that they can work out their differences whilst the rest of the Scrum wasn't watching. Half an hour passes, when the two teams return. Surprised at what he sees, Jax notices that Laurens and Madhuri are sitting beside each other and joking around.

"Is everyone the best of friends again?" he asks, gesturing at the Scrum Team.

"You'd be proud of us, mate. We started thinking about what caused the argument in the first place and realized it wasn't anyone's, really. Look, we've even created a simple working agreement," Ronda points to the place where it's written.

"We do not blame individuals for mistakes because we assume that everyone always tries their best."

Resisting the temptation to explain that they had all just paraphrased the Prime Directive, Jax takes a seat amongst the team. This agreement seems well received by everyone. When they discuss it in more detail, it seem that many of them had been unable to ask each other for help for fear of looking stupid—it felt like a turning point.

Now that they'd moved past that issue, Jax refocuses the conversation on what they are together for. After about an hour, they are finally ready to start the Sprint Retrospective! He asks them to take some sticky notes and write down their most significant problems, happiest moments, and any actionable improvements for the last Sprint. After a round of dot voting, the Scrum Team agrees on what they want to discuss. Unsurprisingly, prompted by John's interruption at the start of their Sprint Retrospective, they choose to talk about why the release was late.

"We were late because there's too much technical debt," Johanna says. "Roy, can we start making it more transparent in the Product Backlog, please?"

"Sure," he says, "we can create time for every Sprint to resolve some of it. How does that sound?" The team nods with tacit approval but also remembers the previous times this had been raised (and nothing changed because Roy was concerned about making it look like his product wasn't perfect). Reading between the lines of the silence, Roy adds, "I know what you're all thinking, but it will be different this time. I promise."

Jax gestures for any other comments about the late release.

"I think we were late because we keep trying to do too much," offers Mackenzie.

"Well, it's my job to ensure I get the most out of the Scrum Team every Sprint!" Roy says defensively, "So, surely, you don't expect me to apologize for that!?"

This conversation continues for ages. Tensions began to rise again, so Jax tries to turn the conversation toward actionable improvements, but the room has no energy. The next topic that got the most votes was "Roy needs to get some proper Product Owner training," but there was no way Jax was opening that can of worms. Silently, without letting the Scrum Team know what he was doing, he ignored the sticky and moved on.

"The Sprint Review was too perfect. We were unwilling to discuss any of the problems we faced in any detail," he reads out. "Okay, so on that thread, assuming we were fully open with our stakeholders, what do we need from them in the future?"

A list is generated that boils down to:

- Clearer requirements
- Update the general market so that we know what to plan for
- Patience when things go wrong
- An understanding that we aren't aiming for perfection
- Support with removing some of our impediments

As they passively work through the list, the concept of a quality level emerges. This leads to a discussion about the Definition of Done.

"Ah! I've been working on one of those for you all," Roy says. "Don't say I never do anything for you. Here you go." He logs into the nearest computer and pulls it up on the screen.

Definition of Done

Relevant documentation is included or updated in three languages: English, Dutch, and French.

User acceptance testing has passed.

Integration tests have passed.

Regression tests are acceptable or above.

Acceptance criteria are met.

Peer review has been performed; critical feedback has been incorporated.

The speed of the product has remained the same.

Unauthorized access is prevented.

Roy is sitting there looking proud of himself. Jax doesn't even have the energy to explain that creating the Definition of Done is a collaborative exercise for the whole Scrum Team.

After all, how do we know if the Developers can even meet it? he thought.

"Ugh. Are we done yet?" groans Mackenzie.

Shortly after her comment, the Sprint Retrospective ends. It may have taken a long time—certainly, there'd been much talking—but nothing happened. Jax knows that the Scrum Team will continue doing the same things in the same way without any improvement. He doesn't want to feel too cynical, but he's been on this merry-go-round before. Everyone leaves feeling emotionally drained. After this experience, it's no surprise that they all hate Sprint Retrospectives.

Where do we go from here?

The title says it all. The fundamental premise of a Sprint Retrospective is for everyone to sit down and discuss what they can do about "it." "It," in this sense, can be anything, from a poorly productive event, an unclear Product Goal, all the way through to an unsupportive team member. Whatever it is, it's your time to get together with your Scrum Team and discuss the *"problemé du Sprint"*—first, by trying to identify all the crocodiles surrounding your canoe and, secondly, by deciding which one to deal with first. Overall, was Magnum Opus' Sprint Retrospective a complete bust? No, it wasn't. Firstly, they actually held one. How often have you worked in "agile" teams that skip the Sprint Retrospective more times than you can count or, worse, don't even have one? The fact that everyone turned up, there was some sense of purpose as to why they were present, and an effort to discuss what occurred in the previous Sprint is positive.

The issues with how you identify the "*problemé du Sprint*" are so numerous that we could write a book on them... hey, what are the chances?! The Sprint Retrospective stands as a beacon of reflection and improvement, but it's often forgotten and completed as a charade of team, self, and organizational improvement. This beacon flickers and fades under the shadow of team arguments, though, turning what should be a constructive session into something resembling a mildly polite (yet chaotic) tea party that no one wants to be at. By reading this book, though, we assume you're one of the valiant people trying to address these anti-patterns. So, we hope you've got the skills of an Agile coach, a diplomat's finesse, a psychologist's insight, and perhaps a saint's patience. In the case of Magnum Opus, we saw a poor environment, disruptive attendees, interpersonal arguments, and lack of engagement, and it is the last one we want to talk about first.

Let's Play a Game...

If you were forced to list the challenges of making Sprint Retrospectives effective, you would be spoiled for choice. Still, often, the perception is that it's solely an issue with the facilitation specifically, that the facilitation is not driving to the root of the real problems faced by the Scrum Team and therefore masking what you're really trying to fix. This could be true in some cases, but ineffective facilitation certainly isn't always the issue. We can't tell you the number of times that we've opened our social media to find that the solution to purposeful improvement is a Mural template themed around a TV show... yeah, good luck with that. Approaches like this are short-term in their attitude because they only look to solve the surface-level issues of engagement (and sometimes even that doesn't work). To use an old metaphor, it's like putting makeup on a pig. We're sorry to tell you that poorly constructed gamification, in our opinion, is hiding the real issue you're facing about why your process isn't improving.

Before going into more detail, we want to say that we *do* see value in utilizing play to support purposeful discussion. The integration of gamification in business contexts has emerged as a powerful tool to enhance outcomes, an idea substantiated by a growing body of academic research. Gamification, applying game-design elements in non-game contexts, leverages intrinsic motivation factors such as reward systems, progress tracking, and interactive challenges to foster engagement and enhance accountability. If you want to know more, the works of Sebastian Deterding are well worth a read (particularly *Game Design Elements to Gamefulness*). This approach is rooted in self-determination theory, which suggests that gamification satisfies human needs for competence, autonomy, and relatedness, thereby increasing motivation toward improvement—isn't this what a Sprint Retrospective is all about? Furthermore, gamified environments have improved cognitive outcomes, meaning you're *smarter* while playing a game—who knew!? Games create a safer space to have tough discussions and also develop what's called a peer-learning environment (which increases interaction). All of these are good things. But... the other side of this argument is what's known as the *Chocolate Covered Broccoli* phenomenon. Gamification may disguise unengaging content without enhancing the participants' deeper understanding or critical thinking skills. Furthermore, the implementation of gamification requires professionalism and training—it's not just pretty colors, a nice picture, and a few questions. They need significant resources and careful design to be effective, with poorly designed Sprint Retrospectives leading to negative experiences, such as frustration or decreased motivation.

Whichever side your opinion falls—whether gamification is awful or amazing—what's missing from the approaches we frequently see is any form of structure, reasoning, or, frankly, logic around how it is done. To combat this, we suggest ignoring the pseudo-science touted by so-called "influencers," avoiding simply downloading a generic template for re-use and differentiating your designs to ensure they meet the moment's needs. Let's talk about the four principles of great retrospection:

Uncompromising Focus on Improvement

The goal is not to make everyone feel good. The goal is not to validate technical discussions as right or wrong. The goal is to make tactical and strategic improvements to a process. This is true for both past and future insights; much like requirements (because that's exactly what they are), improvements should be traceable to a desired impact. You've probably got a Product Goal, so why not a Process Goal? Without an unrelenting focus on doing *something* better, a Sprint Retrospective is without purpose. Everyone needs to be ruthless in treating process improvements as highly as product ones—remember that you're aiming to fix the problem, not the symptom. Forward and backward-looking is ruthless. Don't just treat symptoms. Improvements are just as important as features.

Data-Driven Insights

Like love, financial security, and hunger, process improvements can make you 'feel' a certain way. When we iteratively improve something, it feels good. As a professional, helping your team to identify those feelings is incredibly challenging and has a lot of parallels with relationship coaching (look at *Secure Love* and Julie Mennano if you don't believe us). It is easier to bring data to support reflection against previous action items. If you're wondering how to do that, try using a Strategyzer card. These structure potential improvements and remind you that outcome measurement is important. We all want a 'quick win' from a Sprint Retrospective, and that mentality can often help us to identify low-hanging fruit, but it's also okay to play the long game and aim for sweeping changes that we can impact. Data helps us gauge whether we're on the right track. Remember that while much of your technical debt may be obvious, process debt is the real silent killer of your product.

Test Card
Strategyzer
Log outputs aid bug resolution time
Aug 2024
Alexii
6 weeks
STEP 1: HYPOTHESIS
We believe that ...receiving the log output from a customer's installation...
...will help us to debug their operational bugs 20% faster.
Critical:
STEP 2: TEST
To verify that, we will ...add a new field into our 'Help Form'...
...to request an upload of their log error messages and the version of the software they are currently running.
Test Cost:
Data Reliability:
STEP 3: METRIC
And measure ...the amount of paused time...
...(the amount of time we are waiting for the customer to respond to us with answers) and cycle time for customer resolution.
Time Required:
STEP 4: CRITERIA
We are right if
...the total amount of time to resolve an operational defect decreases (-10% is a positive signal, -20% would be better).
Copyright Business Model Foundry AG
The makers of Business Model Generation and Strategyzer

Figure 39 - An example test card (template available at Strategyzer.com)

Inclusivity as the Foundation

When the same few voices dominate Sprint Planning, the Daily Scrum, the Sprint Review, and everything in between, quieter colleagues are sidelined. While many techniques exist to encourage diverse opinions and comments, teams often defer to a single individual. This person might be the Technical Lead, the Scrum Master, or an experienced developer. Whoever they are, they serve as both an enabler and a hindrance. They enable by injecting energy and enthusiasm into an idea but can hinder it by quickly stifling other contributions. This is why inclusive facilitation is vital; we need to give others the right to shine different perspectives on the past so that they can create unique ideas for the future. Whether opinions are positive or negative, all are valid.

Willingness to be Wrong

Whether the context is personal or professional, everyone has the right to be wrong. Many of us have deep-rooted belief systems that impact our approach to working with others, but without the right attitude, they can cause pain and dysfunction (leading to stagnation and the status quo). Imagine a simple situation where two team members propose different solutions to the same problem—does it really matter whose idea resulted in the best outcome? Accepting that perfection is not a real thing and that flawed ideas are good enough to create a net positive outcome opens the door for every idea to be both wrong and right (at least partially). This idea, System Rule in Organization and Relationship Systems Coaching (ORSC), is fundamental to improving our environment without blame.

Where? When? What? Who? How?

We've all forgotten to book a meeting room at some point. We did a quick search on the internal room booking tool, which revealed a room available (Hallelujah! It's a Sprint-End miracle!), but it's the one in the basement with no windows that smells a little bit like cheese. We lock it in before anyone else books it and send calendar invites. In our story, Magnum Opus booked the Greenhouse, which sounds equally as bad as our cheese-smelling example. Now, before you go to your fridge and grab a piece of cheese (mmm, cheese), we want to talk about how the venue of a Sprint Retrospective can make or break it.

Figure 40 - Reluctantly Jax booked the room.

In many organizations, product teams don't always have a reserved personal room. It will also not be a top-floor, glass-walled experience with a floor-to-ceiling touchscreen display and impressive view. Ignoring impractical measures, some bare minimum expectations should be considered. Privacy, tooling, time of day, and facilitator are all important aspects, and we often default to the easiest options for each.

Where

The most effective Sprint Retrospectives are when the participants are willing to be vulnerable and observe their imperfections. For this to happen, they need a safe space. While we're not going to elaborate on psychological safety (as, frankly, we believe you should only offer advice on things you are ostensibly considered an expert), a safe space is not just physical (privacy for tough conversations) but also conceptual (inclusive, built on positive social norms with growth opportunities). If you've never tried it, go outside and run the event in the sunshine to see the improvements. We're not saying you need to go outside all the time, but having a social, open, and varied location for a Sprint Retrospective can make a huge difference.

Verdict: Somewhere that creates physical and psychological space that enables the team to have difficult conversations.

When

At the end of the Sprint—after the Sprint Review but before the next Sprint Planning. That's the textbook answer. A common event pattern is Sprint Review in the late morning, lunch, then a Sprint Retrospective in the afternoon, with Sprint Planning the following morning. The problem with this in our experience is everyone is knackered after a stressful Sprint Review with the customers. They then follow this with a nice heavy lunch to reward themselves for getting through it and end up wanting an early afternoon nap like a toddler (sweet treats can only maintain a team's energy for so long). We suggest reworking your event calendar so that Sprint Retrospective happens in the morning, precisely when people have the most energy and best hormone balance (called Sleep Inertia, Antony Sanni[25]), enabling us to see more clearly. While a (weaker) peak in our performance is possible in the afternoon, most people don't experience it due to a hectic working pattern.

Verdict: Sprint Retrospectives should happen in the morning.

What

Deciding what to cover during a Sprint Retrospective can be a can of worms. Do you discuss how the last Sprint went concerning individuals, interactions, processes, and tools? You can, but that gets repetitive quickly and leaves a team about as keen to turn up as a guy who knows his wife has a list for him to complete while she's out of town. A logical follow-up question, therefore, is: what is the correct set of topics to cover? You know by now that anyone who tells you a specific answer related to Agile, Scrum, or any complex work is almost always lying to you, themselves, or both of you. The answer, as always, is "it depends." Do you focus on the last Sprint? Maybe that's appropriate based on what happened. Do you focus on something specific, like stakeholder engagement? Maybe, if that's what seems to be a reoccurring issue that never seems to improve. What about the efficacy of the Scrum events? Maybe...you get the picture. The Sprint Retrospective is designed to cover what you need it to cover – the 'last Sprint' is

[25] *https://anthonysanni.com/blog/law-morning-unusual-science-based-facts-morning-special-productivity*

a good place to start, but sometimes you should go wider, sometimes narrower, and sometimes out of the park entirely.

Verdict: Individuals, interactions, processes, and tools are great places to start, but focus on the painful topics that need disruption. A kudos-focused theme is great, but a pat on the back only goes so far.

Who

The Scrum Team. The Scrum Team. And no one but the Scrum Team. If you aren't using Scrum, it should be the people who directly, on a day-to-day basis, impact the work quality, direction, and value. When you're finding yourselves needing introductions at the start of the Sprint Retrospective, then, yeah, you've got the wrong people. Sometimes, consultants and organizations fight this point because they believe that if people want to be there to observe and help, they should be allowed to do so. We disagree—even if a person is so pure of heart that their entire energy is used to serve this team, they still shouldn't be there. Why? Firstly, their presence (even as a silent observer) impacts the conversation and makes it more closed. And secondly, the rest of the team can't be sure their intentions are as pure as they are made out to be. The sad but very real aspect of most modern corporate environments is that people are untrustworthy.

Verdict: The people doing the work on a day-to-day basis, i.e., the Scrum Team.

I ran a Sprint Retrospective for my team in May 2024. It wasn't anything special; in fact, it was a bit of a lazy effort on my part, to be honest. A few years ago, I created a set of Powerful Question cards to give out to participants of my training—so I just brought the deck along, paired the team up randomly, and each pair drew a card. I can still remember the question that my Product Owner and Technical Lead asked; "On a scale of zero to one hundred percent, what level of technical debt does our product have?". Their answer? Seventy-five percent. When the discussion widened to include the rest of the team (and also some downstream technical consumers of the product), the answers ranged from forty–eighty-five percent. The moral of this story is that sometimes, people are willing to talk, but the question needs to be asked in the right format at the right time.

How

For some people, the Sprint Retrospective is a game of psychological warfare. How do you make a team that is happy with the status quo agree to identify and then make improvements? On a famous job application, there is a question that asks, "How could you influence people to make decisions in your best interest?" It's a clever question, no? How do you, as an individual, persuade someone else to do something while getting them to believe it was their idea entirely? The answer, in practicality, is not all that simple.

To share a story that frequents social media, a wonderful product guru, Rory Sutherland (seriously, check him out), worked with a London-based restaurant called Dishoom. Dishoom had a problem; they wanted to be fully booked for lunch but couldn't figure out how to do it. Their owner, Kavi Thakrar, solved the problem by offering breakfast. Why did it work? Well, because at 11/11:30 am, people were still in the restaurant, so, psychologically, people are more willing to enter a restaurant that already has people in it! To relate Dishoom's success (there are so many more stories about this particular Indian restaurant chain that you should look into) to Sprint Retrospectives is to figure out what makes tough discussions more socially acceptable to a Scrum Team. Our suggestion here (as part of good preparation for the Sprint Retrospective) would be to have a series of questions that structure the flow of conversation. Start with some easily accessible ones and then be prepared with some disruptive ones –some people call them pivot, big, devil's, powerful questions—it doesn't matter. Just be ready to use them once the atmosphere is in a good place to receive what would usually be a psychologically unacceptable question.

Verdict: Carefully craft question sequences that intentionally create obstacles. Disruption is most effective in healthy atmospheres.

Now that we've considered the 5 Ws of Sprint Retrospectives, you're good to go. Note that except for "When," none of these have anything to do with Scrum. If you're one of those people who considers the process of retrospection as core to Scrum, then we'd encourage you to reframe your thinking. You're not wrong, but perhaps misguided? Retrospection, the painful art of reviewing the past to enable you to make better decisions in the future, is more analogous to empirical theory. By this, we mean that using retrospection as an activity is core to more than just Scrum—it's the basis of all continuous improvement. Without closing the loop, i.e., taking a transparent view of the recent and not-so-recent history, any team is significantly impeding their ability to improve. Frankly, they are leaving their process improvements down to luck... and as you may have heard before, dumb luck is only one letter away from making you a dumb ****.

Creating a Definition of Done

The final part to address in this chapter (and this seems to be a pattern—why is it always Roy?) is the magical Definition of Done that Roy created for the team. We've reproduced it below to refresh your memory. What do you think?

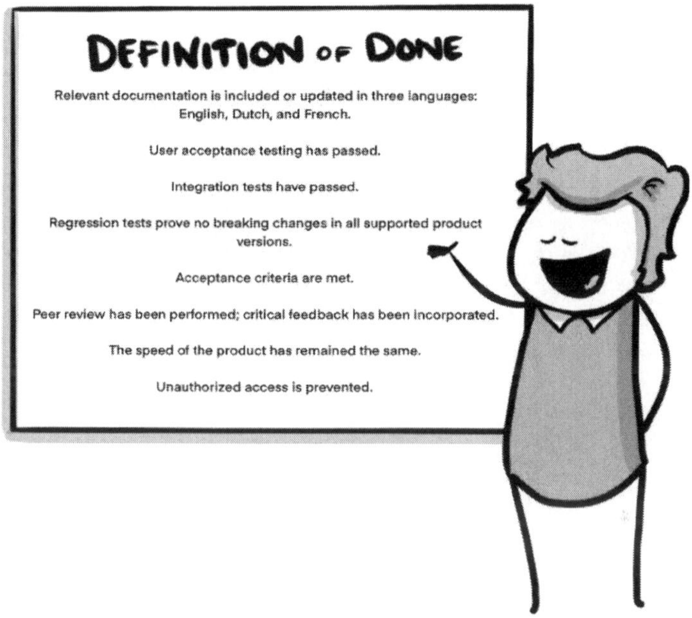

Figure 41 - Roy proudly demonstrates the DoD.

In our opinion, it's not all that bad, right?

- ✓ Binary statements that cover both functional features and non-functional requirements.
- ✓ Not solely focused on development characteristics (such as code coverage) but includes product criteria that customers care about.
- ✓ Almost entirely automatable (to remove the human stupidity of "yeaaaah, that's good enough" release mentality).

Roy hasn't produced a bad Definition of Done here. Sure, it certainly seems designed for a less mature team that is more focused on what they can control, i.e., testing, than more tangible, user-centric quality criteria. Yes, he produced it on his own and delivered it as a finalized commitment instead of a prompt for team discussion. And maybe he could have picked a better time. With all of that said, Roy did something useful by lighting the fire under product quality as the front and center of Magnum Opus' delivery process.

A key aspect of improvement, any improvement, is knowing whether you're looking at a finished piece of functionality or something half-baked. There are so many product teams that we've worked with who do not even have a Definition of Done, and those teams typically have three common characteristics. Firstly, the Sprint boundary means nothing to them; if work carries over, so be it. Secondly, their ability (or willingness) to break work down into manageable chunks is impeded or nonexistent. And finally, they are the teams who say, "Can we just use Kanban instead?"

When a team member said this to me about Kanban, my response was "Sure!" Cut to me arranging a brief overview of how they could define a Workflow, options for calculating their SLA, and even some flow-based metrics we could use to improve pull rate. Within forty minutes, one developer asked if they could just carry on using Scrum because it seemed easier.

If you ask anyone who knows anything about Scrum or complex product development, they will tell you that it boils down to one thing—the concept of Done. Without any formal rules for common inspection, transparency is inhibited and inspection is inconsistent or perhaps worthless, with any resulting adaptation based on incomplete observations. For this reason, beating the Definition of Done drum is a necessary part of improving team dynamics. If they can't even remember it, they'll never leverage it. With that in mind, we want to leave you with two relevant thoughts, one from a legend of Scrum and the other is unattributed. When reading them, we'd encourage you to consider the purpose of a Definition of Done and its rigor in protecting you from poor, in-the-moment choices. Without it, you are ruining any chance of delivering consistent quality to your customers.

"Value rarely scales linearly, but crap scales exponentially." - Rich Hundhausen

AND

"It is far better to consistently conform to a weak Definition of Done than to constantly ignore a strong one." – Unknown

Ryan and Sander's Summary Feed (RSS Feed)

If there are any points that we want you to take away from this chapter, they are as follows:

- The main aim is for the Scrum Team to discuss and address any issues from the Sprint, from productivity problems to unclear goals.
- Identifying issues during Sprint Retrospectives is often flawed, leading to superficial improvements rather than addressing root causes.
- Poorly implemented gamification can mask underlying issues rather than solve them, often failing to improve engagement meaningfully.
- When done correctly, gamification can enhance motivation, foster a safer discussion space, and improve cognitive outcomes, but it requires careful design and significant resources.
- The four principles for effective Sprint Retrospectives are:
    - Focus on Improvement: The goal is to make tactical and strategic improvements, treating process improvements as seriously as product features.
    - Data-Driven Insights: Use data to support reflections and measure the impact of changes, focusing on both quick wins and long-term improvements.
    - Inclusivity: Ensure diverse voices are heard, preventing dominant individuals from stifling contributions and fostering a more collaborative environment.
    - Willingness to be Wrong: Encourage a culture where being wrong is acceptable, facilitating improvement without blame.
- The location can impact effectiveness, with varied, safe spaces enabling more open and honest discussions.
- Sprint Retrospectives should ideally be held in the morning when participants are most alert rather than after a tiring Sprint Review.

- The topics should be flexible, focusing on the most pressing issues rather than sticking to a rigid agenda.
- Only those directly involved in the work (i.e., the Scrum Team) should attend to ensure open and honest discussions.
- Use carefully crafted question sequences to guide discussions, creating opportunities for disruption in a healthy, constructive atmosphere.

Reflection

Use this page to reflect on the initial questions at the beginning of this chapter and what you may have uncovered throughout.

How do you ensure that the improvements identified in your Sprint Retrospectives genuinely address root causes rather than surface-level symptoms?

*How do you **actively** create an inclusive environment during discussions, ensuring that all voices, especially the quieter ones, are heard and valued?*

When was the last time you allowed yourself to be wrong in a professional setting, and how did that experience contribute to your growth or the improvement of your team?

8.

Innovating for Value

"Creativity is thinking up new things. Innovation is doing new things."

–Theodore Levitt

Preflective Questions

Innovation is yet another buzzword that rings the ears of many. We consider that ninety-five percent of the organizations we worked with say they need innovation to survive. And we can't argue with that statement. Where things start to go sideways is the interpretation of innovation. The description of the term differs almost as widely as the description of value. As with many terms, alignment is necessary to interpret innovation and what it entails. We want to be adamantly clear that innovation is essential for survival as a company and should be part of every product team. We have encountered organizations considering removing technical debt, resolving bugs, or working on documentation as innovating. We firmly want to clarify this is not innovating the product or company.

Innovation is the practice of implementing new ideas, products, and companies or adding to existing products or companies to significantly increase their value.

How is your team and organization currently innovating?

How are these innovations aligned with organizational and product strategy and goals?

What darlings should you potentially kill to create more focus?

Ever since Magnum Opus made the switch from traditional project management to working in an Agile fashion, "innovation" has been a recurring buzzword—and one of management's favorites. "If we don't innovate, we'll fall back in the same situation we were in not too long ago!" Larry constantly says. Larry is a Vice President at Magnum Opus but adamantly calls himself CIO, which stands for Chief Innovation Officer, according to him. It might not come as a surprise, but it's a term he innovated for himself.

Larry and the Product Owners at Magnum Opus have regular conversations. During the last few discussions, Larry kept repeating that they have to "Seventy-thirty the backlog!" referring to the idea that seventy percent should be based on maintenance and keeping the product running smoothly, and thirty percent should go to innovation. The problem the Product Owners are currently facing is that no one really knows what innovation means, and, frankly, people are getting sick and tired of hearing the same word over and over. Sarah, the Panda Team's product owner, has been posting memes saying, "Innovation. You keep using that word... I do not think it means what you think it means."

Larry wants to do good work but does not seem to be aligned with the Product Owners in terms of semantics or what kind of work should be done. In theory, time is allocated to the teams to create new solutions to enhance the existing offer. In reality, people in the Scrum Teams feel so overwhelmed and pressured that rarely does anything innovative actually leave their hands.

"Well, why don't you do Friday Pizza Sessions after seven p.m., then?!" Larry opts.

"People don't work like that, Larry," Sarah mentions. "Roy, back me up here. How do you think it would work for your team like that?"

Roy frowns. "Hmm, not sure, really. I mean, they like pizza. But they don't like working after seven. People rarely do. I agree we should keep an eye out for innovation, but I don't think this is the way."

Marge and Jax overhear the three debating while walking by and provokingly ask, "Why should we care about it anyway?" without stopping their pace. Larry looks baffled. In his mind, everyone should know why it is important. People are going to get fired if they don't.

"You look like you've seen a ghost," Roy interrupts his confusion.

"What kind of a dumb question was that?! Why should we care about it anyway?" He repeats the question with a childish voice.

"Well, explain it to us as if we *are* children."

"Listen, if I need to explain to you guys why we should care about innovation, we might just throw our money in the water right away. It's part of your job to ensure that it happens."

"Sure," Roy continues where Larry left off, "but it's the way we ensure that it happens. Forcing people to work overtime will not help the teams' morale. What do you think will happen to the quality of work coming out of forced innovation? If you want to turn into the laughingstock of the biometric security world, be my guest. But I don't think continuing down that path is wise."

After deciding to finish that conversation later, Roy and Sarah return to their teams. After sharing the conversation, the team opts to use the thirty percent time bucket to finish the features they already have in development.

"The stakeholders will receive more features in the same amount of time; I'm sure they'll be happy with that!" Johanna proudly calls out.

Mackenzie and Peter have a different opinion. "That's just the exact same thing as we've been doing right now. Can we accept now calling it differently? How does that ensure the future-proofness of both us as a company as well as the scanners we're making?"

"Well, it ensures that stakeholders have a higher certainty that we deliver what we promise. So, they'll be more inclined to keep buying our stuff, I guess." Johanna takes a defensive argument.

The overheard sigh makes Jax think he's been doing a good job teaching about empiricism, limiting risk, and innovating, as at least half of the team recognize the non-argument Johanna made for herself.

Jax decides this would be a good time to take action and facilitate a session on their definition of innovation and how to pursue it.

To collect individual thoughts, Jax asks everyone on the team to write their single-sentence definition of innovation on a Post-it and stick it to the wall. It appears that the team has a widespread idea of what it means.

"Removing technical debt"

"Adding new features"

"Finishing work in the Sprint Backlog"

"Create new ways to deliver value"

"Enhance the existing product line to delight our customers even more"

"Preventing me from losing my job 😊 "

"Find new ways to solve customer problems"

Then, Googling what it means, they filter out any of their answers that don't align. Ultimately, two tickets remain:

- Find new ways to solve customer problems;
- Enhance the existing product line to delight our customers even more.

Peter can't help but make a fake vomiting gesture to express his opinion about the description. Nonetheless, the team agrees that this would be a good start.

"This isn't even remotely close to what we're constantly being told to do. We're just forced to cram out as much stuff as possible or work that's already in progress. It doesn't seem to have anything to do with innovating our business. I swear, if I hear them telling us to innovate one more time, I will lose it. Seventy-thirty, my ass," Rhonda notes, unambiguous as always.

"Roy, what do you think?" Jax asks, as Roy is accountable for ordering these new services or products in the backlog accordingly. Roy seems to hesitate and pondered his options.

"I'm not sure. I don't disagree with it, but equally I don't know yet how we're expected to get there. How on earth are we going to "delight our customers more"? he air quotes.

"I'm pretty sure we can figure that out. There's a lot of creativity in our team, and we have more than sufficient tools at our disposal. Just look at all the metrics and workshop techniques we haven't used yet, or users we haven't spoken to yet," Jax adds. Jax sometimes feels fatigued having to drag this out of people, but he tries to remember this is what great Scrum Masters do. It takes perseverance to be that person, and that's precisely the person he wants to be.

"So, let's map this out. Let's visualize this and look at where we see opportunities."

The team initially maps out travelers' stages, starting at their homes.

- Online check-in;
- Fingerprint scan;
- Travel to airport;
- *optional* check-in baggage;
- Move to security;
- Have check performed;
- Retrieve personal items;

- Walk over to passport checks;
- Continue.

There's nothing in there that seems out of the ordinary. Airport travel has been the de facto process for forever, and the team feel they aren't likely to change that status quo. Until...

"What if..." Laurens quietly brings up. "We were to use our scanners for health checks while people use them. Can we find any anomalies in their scans? If so, we can open ourselves up to a whole realm of possibilities."

Roy is utterly silent. He doesn't know what to say. It takes a few moments for him to have this idea sink in. "I suppose that does sound amazing. Imagine it would turn out to be real. We would be able to save lives with that. Picture that scenario: Magnum Opus, savior of lives through airport security."

"Yeah, I don't know if that balloon would fly like that," Madhuri notes, but supports Laurens, almost feeling obliged after putting him to shame during *that* Sprint Review. "We need to pitch that idea to John."

Magnum Opus Health

"That has absolutely nothing to do with us," John notes after overhearing the pitch the team did. "BUT there is potential to it. What do you suggest we do now?" he relays the direction to the team.

"We're not sure either. It has, indeed, nothing to do with what we are trying to achieve or our vision. Do we have the skills to create something like this? Absolutely. Does it fall in line with anything we have done or sold before? No. So, what do we do now? What options do we have? This question has been stuck in my mind the entire time after our discussion the other day. We could make an entirely new product, but it would change the company's identity. We could also try to mask it as an additional service, but I'm not sure how much our users would actually appreciate that. We could also decide not to do anything with it at all. But we would miss out on a potentially great opportunity," Roy lay out his thoughts.

It stays quiet for a bit. The whole group seems to think about what to do with it. Laurens hesitantly sparks a tiny seed. "What if... What if we start an entirely new company revolving around healthcare options? Then we could experiment with those kinds of products without hurting the already existing brand."

"Great idea!" John replies. "But on the other hand, I don't think we should expose ourselves to more risk. I mean, I barely got over the heart issues the near-bankruptcy MO went through a while ago. And where are we going to get the people we need?"

Jax suggests creating a minimal business case for it with an overview of costs, risks, potential opportunities, and ROI for John to start working with if desired. And maybe even a little experiment into the current Product Backlog to prove the technology they have created already could be a viable source to build on.

After reviewing the business case, four things happen.

- Laurens breaks with the team to start as the first team with the health products. So, now the team is a man down.
- Based on the business case presented to John, John decides to start a so-called "Innovation team." This team will solely do innovative work and then hand it down to another team that will do more maintenance work.
- Roy is flustered to such a high degree about both these events that he now has no idea how to be open about innovation work out of fear that either someone will run off with their ideas or that he will lose a team member again. He decides to cover this work in their Product Backlog.
- Roy's team's morale tanks, as they feel treated like trash in the can of "cool work." The new team now handles the actual cool things. They lost all of Laurens' experience, and they leave with maintenance work, leaving out all their creativity. Something has to change—again.

Where do we go from here?

Often, people don't exactly know what they want to convey with the term innovation. Innovating for the sake of innovating is not going to help. In fact, it will lead you to create an active scrapyard of products in your organization without even realizing it. Not thinking about why, if, and how to innovate is nothing more than providing occupational therapy for the zombies we referred to earlier in this book. They're running in circles around a product that will be terminated shortly anyway. Killing your darlings, like features in the backlog, is one of the hardest things to do. Google is known for terminating a ton of different products. So much so, there's a website listing what products and services have been killed at the monopolous company. https://killedby.tech/google/ currently shows over 450 of Google's discontinued products. We're sure there's a new addition to the list by the time these letters reach your eyes. The beautiful thing about creating such a graveyard is that we can actively track how much we have saved the organizations.

The sunk-cost fallacy is when people or organizations are reluctant to abandon their current strategy only because of the investments that have already been made (usually pretty substantial), even though it is clear that it would be more beneficial to the organization to discontinue the current path. An example of the sunk-cost fallacy is the *Concorde* supersonic airplane. Although it was clear that the high-tech flying tube was already six times more expensive than initially estimated and budgeted, the amount of fuel needed to operate and ticket prices were staggeringly high; the French and British governments insistently decided to continue developing the innovative machine. Besides that, there were many complaints about the noise when it would go supersonic over densely populated areas. One of the biggest benefits of this machine would also become one of the biggest limitations.

Tying it to a goal or a problem that needs to be fixed will get organizations a lot further. Rather than jumping the gun blindly, we need to think about our options. This chapter provides a few options when dealing with situations like Roy's and the team's. Before discussing the options, consider the "why" first. Remember: start with 'why'.

Another example of the sunk-cost fallacy in my personal life was when I was watching the series "Dexter." By far one of my favourite shows at that time. I would be anticipating every new episode up until the last two seasons. Those felt like an absolute drag to me, but I also didn't want to abandon the show had I watched for over seven seasons. Continuing down to the very end, the last seasons felt like negative ROI. I could have jumped ship, but I didn't because of all the other seasons I already watched.

Why is innovating important? First, someone else will innovate for you if you don't do it. And then you end up in the same position Magnum Opus was at the beginning of this book. And second, to create a better user experience with your brand or company. We can't always sit around with the same product in the same state. The human species at large would have been nowhere if we had not innovated our ways of utilizing tools to catch prey, make fire, or build a shelter. That process is never-ending. Life right now is different than it was thirty years ago. And thirty years into the future, life will be different again.

Similarly, putting innovation work in a single team and the day-to-day tasks into another team might not go over well either. We're not saying it doesn't work, but think it through. Ideally, a single product team is fully accountable for the entire product lifecycle. This also means innovation, maintenance, and decommissioning. Often, this is perceived as "unproductive." The reality is that it is often less desirable to have separate teams for individual phases, such as a Discovery Team, Development Team, Innovation Team, etc. Some people may not thrive well on the unknown of innovation or the continuity of maintenance work. Additionally, having separate teams, as mentioned, creates more handovers, complicates communication, and increases dependencies. Now, let's talk about a few options for how to work with innovation.

Do Nothing

Listen (or read, actually). We're not saying this is the *best* option, but it is *an* option. Again, we need to be aware of the options we have available to utilize them in the first place. Not doing anything can be useful when your product or organization is in a comfortable place where it has become your cash cow, and you can milk it. While we advise always focusing on quality first, maybe something of lesser quality has snuck in on your path to product dominance. Remove technical debt or bugs, even though they *technically* should not be there. Technically. But we know theory and practice often differ vastly. How it should be vs real life. We've been there. Do be aware that your cash cow doesn't bleed out. We have seen too many companies that actively stabbed their cash cow to death without doing it deliberately.

Figure 42 - Don't keep milking your cash cow until it's beyond giving.

Enhance the Existing Product

Creating new features or enhancing the existing ones in our product is primarily profitable in products that have not yet become (full-grown) cash cows. The investment required versus the ROI still makes sense at this point. A great model for thinking about product innovation is the Kano model (Kano, 1984).[26]

A product or service will only be successful if it effectively solves one or more important customer problems. –KanoArticle2013

As Dr. Phil says, "Perception is reality." The Kano model helps you measure and explore customers' emotional responses to products or features. This can help us in our continuous journey. This tool works well when we have no particular evidence that a feature or product might support our customer base. This supports the discovery process discussed earlier in this book. Not every idea is equally valuable. Some ideas might even regress the value your users are experiencing from your product—for example, the transition from Windows 7 to Windows 8. Windows 8 had a vastly different interface, which most of the user

[26] Kano, 1984.

base was unfamiliar with. This decreased sales and adoption rates, ultimately influencing Microsoft to incorporate a more traditionally influenced interface for its next launch.

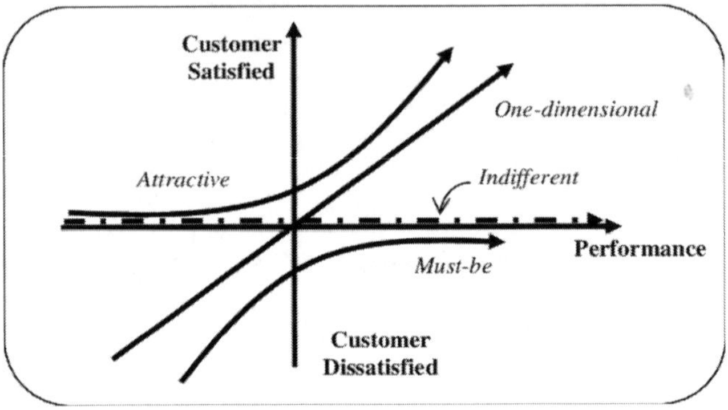

Figure 43 - Kano model (Kano, 1984)

Kano hypothesized five emotional response types to features:

1. Must-be (or must-have) features;
2. Performance features;
3. Attractive features;
4. Indifferent features;
5. Reverse features.

The model displays two main axes with five respective levels of scale:

- (Functional) Performance (horizontal)
  - None
  - Some
  - Basic
  - Good
  - Best
- Customer satisfaction (vertical)
  - Delighted
  - Satisfied
  - Neutral
  - Dissatisfied
  - Frustrated

Based on the Kano questionnaire, we can now map features on the Kano scales.

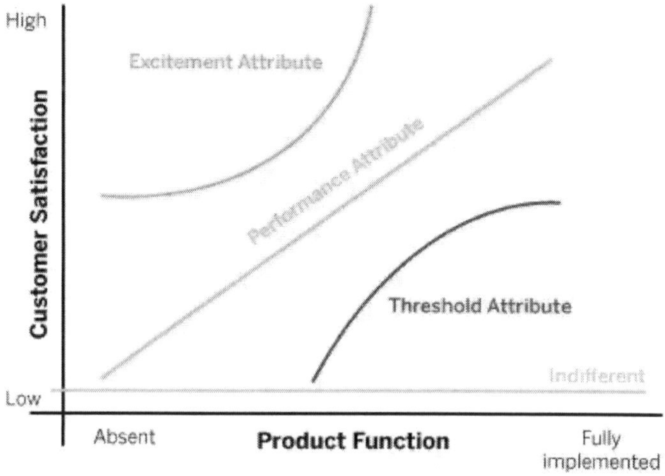

Figure 44 - Levels of Attribution.

Then, we can categorize five different types of features and their response.

Requirements type:	Summary:
Must-be	Basic expectation. It doesn't delight the customer, and it frustrates them when absent. Example: a pillow in a hotel bed.
One-dimensional (Desired quality)	More is better. The more these criteria are met, the more likely the customer will be satisfied. Example: streaming service on the hotel TV.
Delighters (Exciters)	It does not cause frustration upon absence, yet it will delight the customer when present. Example: a complimentary bottle of champagne in the hotel room.
Indifferent	The customer doesn't care whether or not the feature is present. Example: the brand of showerhead in the hotel room.
Reverse	Causing dissatisfaction when present. Example: painfully slow or unstable Wi-Fi connection.

As with all models and templates in this book, the mapping is prone to change over time. What may be a delighter today is the must-be a year from now. This is also one of the biggest dysfunctional yet persistent arguments we have encountered in consulting:

We've always done it like this, so why change now?

– Random non-contributor to change

It took us a solid hour to write this single sentence without feeling the tendency to throw up. The first time people started placing glass in windows was around 100 AD. Around 1934, it was the first time recorded in history that double-layer glass windows were used. Since then, many different new layers with various degrees of insulation have been added. The fact that we have had a single-layer glass business for over 1800 years does not make it a valid argument not to change.

Ensuring your product's innovation is essential to its long-term success and viability. Without innovation, you're a sitting duck for competitors to take over your spot. Equally, only focusing on innovation makes you miss out on optimizing for current usage. As with everything, finding the balance is key. But make sure that innovation is consistently part of your development process. We've worked with teams that did two to three work items every week dedicated to innovation, and we've had teams that thrived well on hackathons and innovation days. Find out what works best for you and your product team, but at least ensure it happens and people know it.

Create a New Product

What if the idea doesn't align with your Product Vision or Goals? It might still be highly valuable. It may just become the cash cow when appropriately treated and deemed usable and valuable by the market. For example, something new arose in Magnum Opus that had nothing to do with the original product line. However, it still may be a great idea. Laurens went rogue and just jumped on the opportunity. Sometimes, this may prove to be correct. In more cases than not, it doesn't.

Creating an experiment in the existing team can be a workable solution to lower the risk of overinvesting time, money, or resources and identify whether it is worth more investments. That could be as simple as conducting a survey and interviewing potential users and stakeholders or creating some (paper) prototypes to validate assumptions. If it seems there is potential value, then starting a new team around the new product may be helpful. Don't go haywire and immediately plunge twelve teams into something that doesn't have a solid foundation yet. At this point, you can return to the beginning of this book to fire up the development. Nail it before you scale it—more on scaling in Chapter 9.

Start a New Company

Sometimes, a new idea doesn't fit the product or the company strategy. If the new idea is valuable, and we potentially make it profitable/valuable to our stakeholders or society, we can spin up an entirely new company. This has the benefit of creating focus, both for the new company and the original one. Many companies produce more products than they should.

> *"More businesses die from indigestion than starvation"* – David Packard

This quote emphasizes precisely why it is essential to focus and not overpopulate the portfolio with more clutter. More products mean less focus, which means less quality. Less quality leads to lower customer satisfaction, leading to less revenue. It's a death trap for organizations. *The Lean Startup* by Eric Ries is a great resource for creating a new, lean, focused organization. What we have experienced as another benefit of this strategy is that it can potentially mitigate the risk of competitors with your corporate group. Imagine the following scenario.

Figure 45 - Starting a new company can be a great option to spread risk and capitalize on opportunities.

Magnum Opus has established itself as a dominant player in the market and is now the incumbent. In many cases, the more established a company becomes, the more selective it becomes with its clientele. "We only work with Fortune 250 companies." This inherently also means that Magnum Opus has eliminated an ocean of potential clients to work with, leaving those for other companies to feed on. Entrants to the market can capitalize on this opportunity to accelerate their growth and challenge the incumbents. Like DJ Khaled's album, Magnum Opus is now suffering from success.

This, in many cases in our experience, is for various reasons. These include:

- The original company has created too many overhead layers, making it impossible to adapt quickly.
- The threat isn't imminent enough until it is. And then it is too late.
- Too little focus due to the overpopulated portfolio.
- Failure to innovate.

Harvard's *Disruptive Strategy*[27] supports our experience but goes beyond what is described above. Disruption goes beyond the established products and does something completely different. The example mentioned above speaks of existing markets, whereas market disruption speaks of opening completely new markets like by now classic examples like Uber[28] and Lyft.

Additionally, not every new idea is equally great. If we can't:

- Enhance the existing product;
- Create a profitable/viable product;
- Create a new business.

It might be better not to act on this idea. You might be creating a new Concorde. We have created a decision-making tree to help you guide your actions on the next page. Reiterating our repetitive words throughout this book: nothing replaces critical thinking, inspection, and adaptation.

[27] *https://hbr.org/2015/12/what-is-disruptive-innovation*

[28] *Cramer & Krueger,* Disruptive Change in the Taxi Business: The Case of Uber

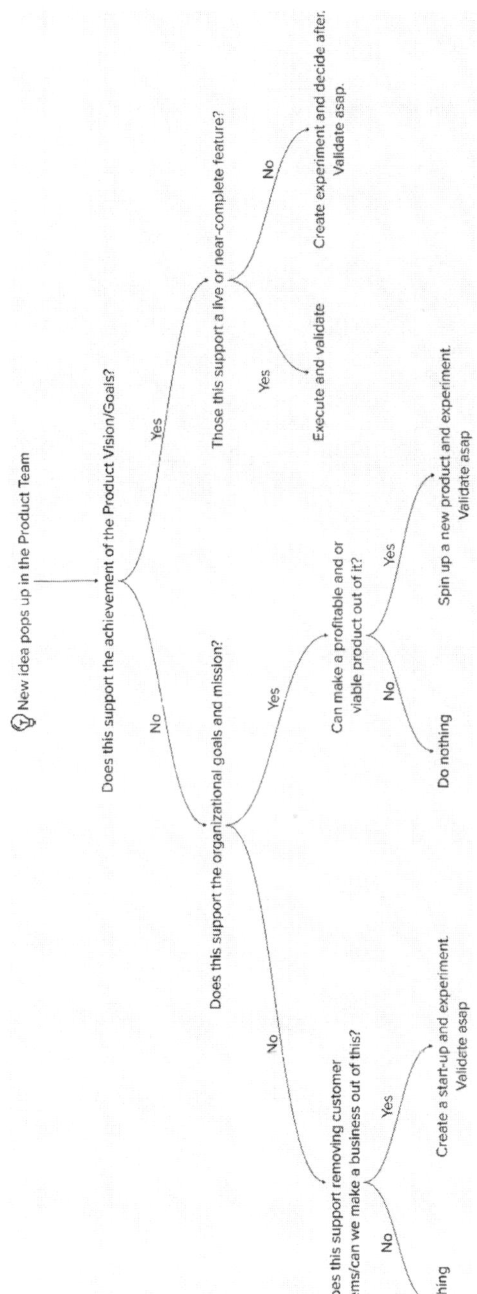

Figure 46 - Innovation decision-making tree.

Ryan and Sander's Summary Feed (RSS Feed)

If there are any points that we want you to take away from this chapter, they are as follows:

- Innovation often is *not* what people think it is and needs proper thought to put into practice.
- How and what to innovate requires alignment with the product or the organization.
- Without understanding our stakeholders' needs and desires, we can deliver negative value, decreasing their happiness.
- Innovation brings risk. Always. Measuring outcomes is essential to continue value delivery.
- Even though innovation is a choice, the consequences of *not* innovating can be dire. We expose ourselves to a higher risk of competitors outperforming us or, worse, finding new markets before we do.
- Focusing too much on innovation can lead focus away from maximizing the outcome for our current product.

Reflection

Use this page to reflect on the initial questions at the beginning of this chapter and what you may have uncovered throughout.

How much of your team's capacity currently gets spent on innovation?

What sources are used to innovate?

What features or products are your competitors delivering that your team or organization could benefit from?

9.

Scaling for Value

"The essence of strategy is choosing what not to do."

– Michael Porterer

Preflective Questions

Modern scaling seems to be a synonym for only two things:

- Adding more people;
- Throwing the blanket of a scaling framework over an already existing large group of people.

The reasons for "scaling" are often well-intentioned but poorly executed *and* misunderstood. *"But we have to keep people busy, right?"* Wrong. That's just limited, putting the busy in business. Being busy does not equate to being effective or valuable. In our experience, scaling frameworks often do more harm than good when mapped to an existing organization without making appropriate changes. That's leaving out the fact that your foundation should be in order first before you *scale up*. If you scale up sh*t, you only get a bigger pile of sh*t. We'd even go as far as to state that scaling up should be your last resort. Only when all other options have been tried and tested do you have a solid foundation, and if you still need to go bigger, is it viable? Scaling up should be as lean as possible, including your product, backlog, and agenda.

How many teams work simultaneously on your organization's product(s)?

What has been the argument for scaling up, if any?

What alternatives were/are available?

The team has been working together for nine months and has been experiencing success. The scanner they've created is being adopted widely, and stakeholders are happy.

John has been keeping an eye on the impact of this team. He's proud to see their results and feels it was time to go to the next level. He plans a meeting in the agendas of all the team members for next week's Tuesday, something that disrupts most people's plans. Upon inquiring what's going on, they only receive back from John, "I specifically listed it as a very important topic. I require everyone to free up their schedules for this one."

The team joins the meeting with high reluctance and low energy. Everyone berates the problems caused by this sudden "move-all-or-else" attitude.

"I can tell by the looks on your faces that you are not happy being here," John starts positively. "However, I want to take a look back in time with you all. Roughly ten months, to be specific. The board and I had given Roy the glorious task of preventing this company from going bankrupt and saving people's jobs. And today, I am standing in front of you saying: you did it. We made it. We are so incredibly proud of you."

The team's eyes light up, and the energy starts to come back. Not for long, though.

"That's why we've decided that in two months from now, the entire company will jump on the path you've paved. You've all demonstrated to be true leaders. Everyone will be working on the entire new line of products, and we need your experience to train everyone. This will skyrocket our revenue, allowing us to grow beyond our original dominant position. We need a scaling framework. And probably something AI, too. Everyone else is using AI, so why do I never see us do that? Adopting that at the same time sounds like a good idea. I don't want to fall behind on the competition again just because we're missing out on the stuff they are doing."

"But hold on," Jax interrupts. "How do you expect us to continue our work and train all the other 240-odd people? Surely you can't be serious with this."

"Why not? You've had bigger challenges. In fact, I need you, Jax, to work with Marge to manage people into the right teams. You guys know how to build teams. So, our idea is to collect your input and start with the new teams in two months."

Jax has trouble channeling his thoughts. Despite enjoying the acknowledgments of their success and outcomes, everyone riding the hype train seems like a guaranteed downfall. And where did Artificial Intelligence come from? Does John even realize what it's used for? After listening to the team's apprehension and fears, Jax goes over to Marge to strategize for the expansion of teams.

"What if we just list the product line, its goals, and the skills needed per product, then gather everyone in the auditorium and have them map themselves across the initial teams?" Marge coins. "Given the self-managing nature, this just sounds the most logical and the first step in creating a sense of ownership and autonomy."

Jax loves the idea. He adds that everyone should list the top three preferred products for everyone to work on so there will be options to work with rather than having everyone sign up for a single team. He and Marge will iron out the bumps wherever needed or provide support when the organization goes south. Before the scaling event takes place, they ensure a Product Owner is appointed for every product in the line. This ensures that everyone can ask their questions about what needs to be built and is provided with the insights available then.

Now, there are six products, with each a dedicated Product Owner:

- Iris Scanner – Roy
- Hand palm geometry scanner – Sarah
- Voice recognition – Tom
- Facial recognition – Maryna
- Retina scanner – Bob
- User portal, connecting all of the above – Juan

The event is received very well. People enjoy themselves, have concerns, and feel it's a great way to feel heard and organize it in this particular way. After listing their top three products they would love to work on, everyone goes home, leaving Jax, Marge, and the Product Owners with the challenge of organizing people's preferences into actual teams. It takes them a good day, but they, too, are happy with the results. They present their idea back to the rest of the company, and apart from a sole voice, the Magnum Opus employees are satisfied with the results.

Then an email pops up from the board, saying they would move some people around—against their own preferred options. The energy and enthusiasm built up over the past few days immediately drops.

"Why did we manage ourselves into teams if the board just comes in and destroys it anyway? One developer mentions. Other frustrations are voiced.

"What kind of nonsense is this? If they know better, why didn't they organize the event?"

"Why did I even expect differently? It's always the same with these people..."

Jax and Marge can understand the absolute disgruntlement. The whole purpose was pulled from underneath them like a rug. Maybe it's the inexperience of management, or maybe it's their anxiety about not feeling in control. Maybe it's something else, but it definitely does more harm than good. It takes them two weeks to figure out the next steps. A reset is made to the initial plan, *but* Jax and Marge will need to be the Scrum Masters for all new teams that haven't got an experienced person for the job as well. This means both of them go from one single team to five teams each. To make matters worse, the teams aren't even working on the same product.

"Same difference. It's all still the exact same, except now on steroids. I can't wait to burn out!" Marge sarcastically mentions.

Three months later, management sits down with the Product Owners and Scrum Masters.

"We've been looking at the progress we've been making. It's not what we expected. Productivity is up compared to the individual team we started with, but given the fact that we've increased the number of people working on this specific line of products by almost three thousand percent, we had set the target to have at least two thousand percent increase in performance as well."

"Gee, who would have thought?!" Jax passive-aggressively adds, realizing he didn't contribute to a good debate.

"Then tell us what's going on. Why are these results not as we expected?" John wants answers.

"More people does not equate to the same amount of increased productivity. In fact, if you look at the iris scanner team, our beloved success story, they have definitely gone down in their productivity by almost ninety percent. You've asked us to train all the other people, meaning we've barely got any time left to develop anything. And *when* we're actually developing, we constantly get interrupted because something allegedly urgent comes up. We're fighting an uphill battle because we did a Big Bang-style scaling approach. It's opening a can of worms."

Maryna chimes in, supporting Jax. "And you need to consider that the new teams need to get up to speed with the product, the stakeholders they knew nothing or very little about, and so on. It's an unrealistic and unfair expectation to have of us new teams. We are not the same team as Roy and Jax'."

"You guys all know what to build, right? That's what we hired you for, for crying out loud."

"Your job isn't to meddle with our team composition either, is it?" Tom adds, almost setting off a major argument.

Marge jumps in before they all begin shouting at each other and nothing constructive gets done. "We have the skills to figure out what to build, indeed. But that doesn't take away the complexity of the products, the market, the competition, and all the other variables we need to consider. It's not a straightforward approach for these machines. If it would have been, we wouldn't have been on the brink of bankruptcy a while ago. And if that wasn't bad enough already, on average, the teams have 533 Product Backlog items they need to do within the next half a year."

John and the other directors understand Marge's perspective. Yet they still have to do their jobs, so they need the scaling effort to succeed.

"So," John wants to move on before losing his cool. "I've been looking around at what other organizations have been doing. The majority seem to be applying that SAFe thing. I think we should go for that, too. That is supposed to create alignment across all teams."

Jax has to do his best to hold his most primal screams. "You're now doing the exact same thing Roy did at the beginning of our Scrum implementation. You're trying to force a framework in that you don't have a clue about how it works."

John disagrees. "We have you guys now. You have all the experience with Scrum, which is at the heart of SAFe, or so I have heard. You're just overcomplicating things. Let's try and see what happens. I'm sure with the experience we have now, we can make magic happen again."

Roy can't help himself and rolls his eyes out of frustration but also because he's now served with an extremely hindsight mirror on his own behavior. He can finally see how hard it must have been for people to follow along with his idea and clueless approach at the beginning of their long journey.

<u>*Where do we go from here?*</u>

Applying a scaling framework to a substantial development effort can be tricky. When a legacy organization has just let the effort grow without keeping things lean, the scaling framework will probably become a painful display of dysfunctions and redundancies. Two things are likely to happen:

- Continue with the existing organization, accepting that expected benefits are unlikely to happen;
- Reorganization of the department/product hierarchies, causing all sorts of anxiety, potentially leading to lowered outcomes and quality.

Half-assed implementations of any framework or methodology are like building your house on quicksand. Initially, things seem fine until the lack of foundation causes your new structure to sink. This is also why this chapter is almost at the end of this book. Scaling up can only follow after ensuring the initial smaller-scale development efforts are adequately done before moving on to the next.

"But how long should we work before scaling? We need to get things done right now!"

It depends. We can't answer that question. Yes, we know that answer is useless to you, so, let us provide some arguments for our consultant's answer. First and foremost, we don't work in your organization, so we don't know your context.

"What does that have to with it?"

As mentioned earlier, there are no best practices in Agile development. What worked for us may not work for your organization. Or maybe it does. It depends. What we *can* do is provide some different options again for you to experiment with. Bear in mind that you scale up the budget, communication lines, and integration coordination required by scaling up the effort. Impediments at scale are more impactful, too. Adding more people adds more complexity. Adding more people to a project that is already late will make it even later. The new people need to get accustomed to the product, the people, and even the organization and its policies if they are new to the organization. We already mentioned this a few times before thinking about what *not* to do might be the best option. Descaling can prove to be your most viable scaling option. The first option should always be to take it to the team and ask them to solve it. If there are challenges or the team doesn't find any solutions, allow us to provide some ideas in this chapter.

The most extreme case of blind scaling I have experienced was working in a particularly dominant, globally present organization that required the entire organization to apply SAFe. They were not looking at local problems, challenges, preferences, and so on but required all three thousand-plus employees to work in the same framework. The department that I worked with had roughly four hundred people. No actual changes were made in the department; everyone just got a new, shiny title and then called themselves an Agile Organization. The implementation was suboptimal at best, and people were highly confused. Dependencies were visualized and then left to be ignored. It was one big confusion, but now with brand new names.

Descaling

Descaling can be as easy as removing things from your backlog, removing redundancies in people or resources, or the amount of teams. The difference between lowering the number of people involved and the number of teams is that the number of people can remain stable when merging two or more teams for efficiency. Let's break that down into some examples.

The old Pareto rule is still upheld in most organizations we've worked with. Eighty percent of the value delivered is derived from twenty percent of the work. Those numbers don't have to be exact, but the idea remains the same. Suppose the vast majority of the revenue or perceived value by the customer comes from the minority of the work. Should we truly be working on the remaining eighty percent of ideas? Or can we be more efficient if we do *not* do that work? Here's a simple example:

Imagine that Roy's team has completed one hundred thirty-six work items in the last six months. Out of those completed work items, only twenty-eight proved to be truly valuable. It took the team almost four Sprints to complete these, roughly seven weeks, rendering them basically four full months that could have been spent differently, for instance, by innovating the product or developing new products. We know correcting after the work has been delivered is easy. If we knew everything upfront, Sander probably wouldn't have taken that eighth vodka shot. Again. It's now the trick to discover what works and what doesn't. What features are being used and which ones are not? And, as this is a chapter about scaling, consider what products to either descale or remove from your portfolio. The investment required to deliver either features or products can now be spent on other things that have proven to deliver value or to run experiments with.

To clarify, by limiting the number of people, we do not mean to fire them. They might have some very useful skills to put into practice in other products or experiments. Firing them, especially at scale, is rather costly. According to Bloomberg[29] Meta Platforms Inc. laid off eleven thousand employees in 2022 and paid a staggering $975 million in severance costs. With these numbers, we can tell you that it is over $88,000 per (now ex) employee. Those costs are not only material. Some of the remaining employees struggled with anxiety and low morale. Some even quit, resulting in additional costs to hire and train the people needed to replace those not part of the layoff. Laying off people often brings additional costs that were initially unable to be precisely forecast. Lower morale leads to lower quality, costing more time (and therefore money) to deliver a valuable product. And isn't that precisely what we want to do (answer: yes, it is)?

Descaling the workload in your backlog or portfolio starts with inspecting two things:

- What is our goal?
- What, out of all our work items or products, do we *genuinely* need to achieve that goal?

Organic Scaling

If you followed our advice in the previous paragraph (if so, sweet) and still feel the need to scale up, organic scaling is the leanest way. We can compare that to a person trying to build muscle. Someone like that needs to eat more; his base metabolism is to feed the muscles, but overeating will result in excess fat levels. To prevent losing you as a reader, here are some numbers to make it easier.

Bob, from the Retina Scanner, wants to build muscle. If he does absolutely nothing, his body burns 2500 calories per day. Depending on activity levels, his body burns more calories. He goes to the gym five times a week, resulting in a basic need of 2700 calories daily for body composition maintenance. In other words, if Bob's team wants to deliver absolute basic functionality, he would need

[29] *https://www.bloomberg.com/graphics/2024-cost-of-layoffs-quantified/*

his regular team of seven people. But Bob doesn't want to provide basic functionality; he thinks he can do better.

If Bob wants to grow muscle, he will need ten to fifteen percent above his maintenance to add lean muscle, given his current body composition. But as he grows, his body will need more food to sustain that growth. So, over time, Bob will need to increase his intake gradually based on the results he achieves. However, if Bob is greedy and starts eating six thousand calories, the moment bodybuilding stops, he will get fat rapidly, and his arteries will clog up. That is no different when doubling or tripling (or even worse) the number of teams currently working on the product. Especially when keeping the original team in the same composition.

That may sound counterintuitive because they now have all these new people to work with, right? Wrong! If the original team has a good flow of work, and the new teams cannot consume that flow because they have to adjust to the new context, product, etc., there is an excess of work that now goes nowhere. A competitive, experienced bodybuilder can consume six thousand calories a day, while a regular, starting person cannot. In the case of Bob, that would result in fully loaded backlogs for the new team, which only keep increasing.

"Why on earth are you comparing fitness to product development? They're completely different things!"

Yes, but no. There are many parallels between nature and solving complex problems. The evolution of species constantly responds to changing circumstances. So, the reality is that there are quite a few things we can learn from looking at nature and how we can use those aspects in product development. Like many people in fitness, some hate looking in the mirror, often the starting point of a wonderful journey to a healthier situation. We need to build gradually, as lean as possible, to keep things healthy and without excesses. That's not always possible, but it creates a solid foundation.

Let's take these lessons back to organic scaling before we drift off into even more tangents than we already have elsewhere in the book. A solid foundation in the case of product teams starts with elements discussed in previous chapters:

- Clear goals;
- Experience in the framework of choice;
- Clear stakeholders;
- Ability to rapidly learn and apply.

We can start forming a new team when these elements are in place. Bob's team currently consists of seven people.

Let's ask two of those people, preferably highly experienced people, and have them self -manage a team around them. What we can't do is have two people move; that would leave such a gap that the remaining five members would collapse. So, we need solid experience with the whole team.

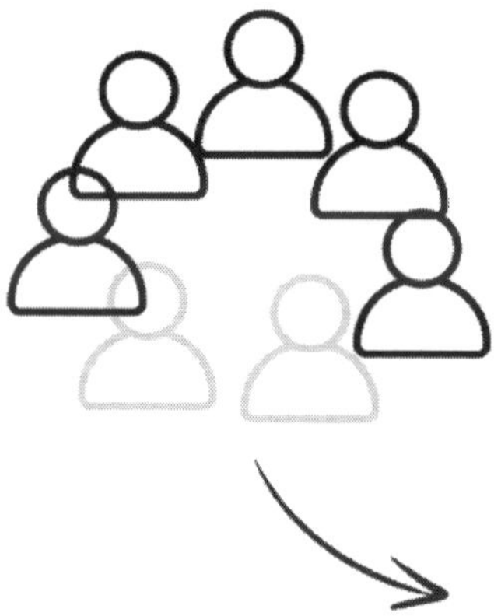

As the original team still needs a sufficient number of people to continue their work, we need to hire new people for both the new and original teams. Note that removing or replacing people will *always* have a (finger-crossed that it's temporary) dip in productivity. This is also another dysfunction. Many organizations seem to expect that a few knowledge transfer sessions with new people are sufficient to "let them hit the ground running." We're sorry to burst the bubble; they are not running. They're barely crawling. They're being flooded with information over the span of two months and are expected to digest all of it without any issues. Knowledge comes from experience. Unfortunately, we can't copy-paste the experience.

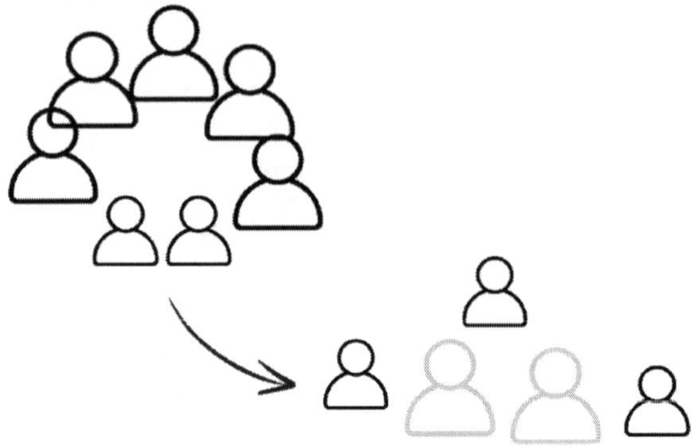

Bob also needs to shift his position slightly because he now needs to work with two teams. A product can have only one Product Owner or Product Manager, so Bob now works with both teams. Bob does not become the messenger between teams. Developers can and should communicate between teams where needed or requested.

Keep repeating this until there are sufficient people involved without making communication too complicated. This ensures a lean approach with valuable outcomes. Eventually, Bob needs twenty-five people to deliver the retina scanner. If these people would like to switch products or teams, we suggest having a look into Heidi Helfand's work *Dynamic Reteaming.*[30] This book dives into the benefits

[30] *https://www.heidihelfand.com/dynamic-reteaming/*

of having team members join other teams when they feel it would help either them, the team, or the organization.

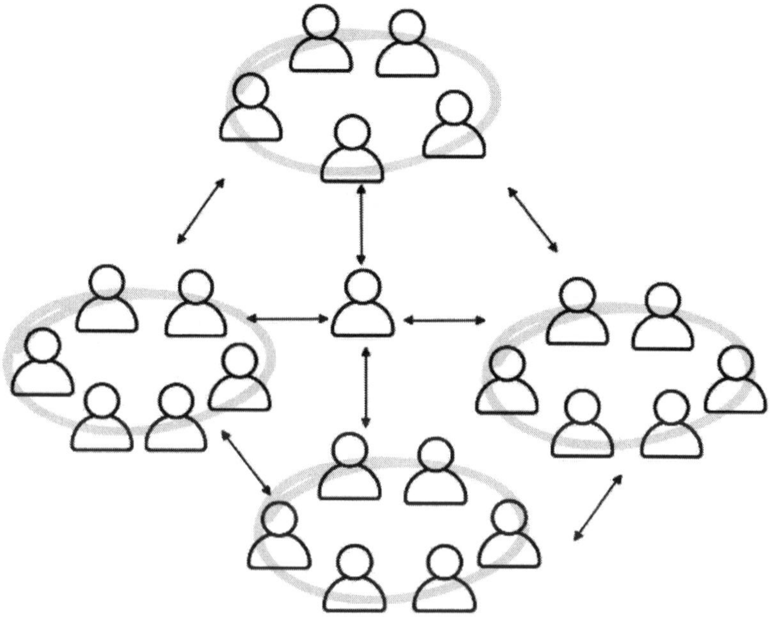

"All fun and games, but we don't have time to upscale that slowly. We need to deliver, stat!"

Then, we would like to refer you to the Descaling part of this chapter. We can almost guarantee you that opening a few cans of developers only results in lowered results at worst and minimal results at best.

One of the many dysfunctions we have seen in scaling is calling everyone a Product Owner. Every team has a different Product Owner, yet they all work on the same product. There is a very simple way to figure out who the real Product Owner is: find the one who can overrule all decisions, and that's the person you need.

"But they are not part of the development! They're higher managers."

Then they must transfer the decision-making authority to someone involved in the development. Otherwise, it will take developers forever to make a decision. Before you know it, micromanagement sneaks in, and then we're only adding ~~fat~~ fluff to the development.

Figure 47 - Prevent the all-seeing micromanager from overruling the Product Owner.

Celling

Another way of creating more cohesion is through cells. Cells, similar to guilds, tribes, and other forms of creating focus, can span multiple offerings and departments yet work on the same product. An example of this can be seen in consultancy firms that offer various services, like consultancy, training, development, etc. These cells are much like feature teams and component teams but have been added with some additional constraints. A cell can offer multiple products to clients. Cells cannot work alone as a single unit in an organization; they have to collaborate with others. Because cells don't have individual Profit and Loss, they are easier to spin up and dismantle again when things don't work as envisioned.

Dedicated Cells

A dedicated cell focuses on specific traits like training, consulting, or management. Let's take training as an example of a dedicated cell.

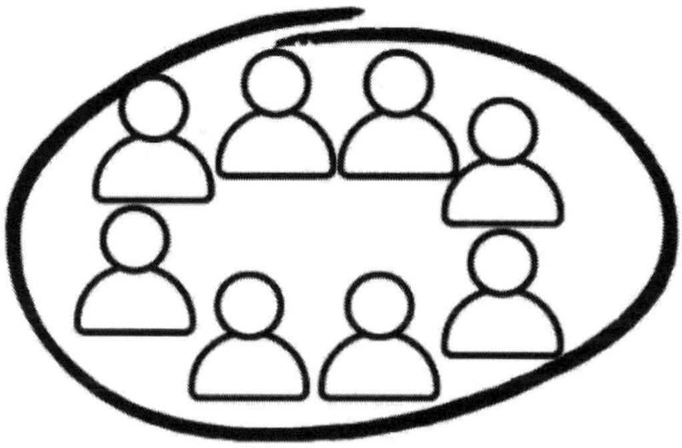

Everyone in this cell is a trainer, so they can support each other in getting better. Their training portfolio can be a wide variety, for instance:

- Product Management;
- Leadership;
- Stakeholder Management;
- Scrum;
- Scaled Agile frameworks;
- Architecture;
- Security;
- Team Building;
- Etc.

Together, the portfolio supports clients in building a stronger, more aligned organization. The upside of a dedicated cell is that trainers can truly hone their craft and have a wide variety of training areas on offer. However, their strength can also be a downside: lowered focus might occur. There, too, the Pareto rule can be applied.

Topic Cells

Topic cells consist of a mixture of skills related to the same topic. Let's take Product as an example. They can have both consultants and trainers on board, which allows them to put the theory into practice and vice versa. That means the training portfolio is reduced to only the topic-related courses to increase focus.

Within this specific topic, the cell members can excel (pun definitely intended). This increased connection to the workspace has the benefit that the gap to the market is shorter. A trainer-focused cell might lead to trainers failing behind on the developments in the field. Consultants can try something, see the results, and feed that back to the trainers to keep the course material relevant. However, in many organizations, the compensation rates of trainers and consultants differ vastly, which might become a dealbreaker.

Cell Support

Neither of these can do all this work alone; they need additional support from sales, marketing, and management to stay healthy. Sales need to go to the market and sell the offerings, marketing needs to create content awareness, and management supports these teams by providing the environment to thrive and aligning with them on how the current offering fits into the organizational strategy. Note that they do not manage the offering of the cells, but both management and cells align on how to stay focused.

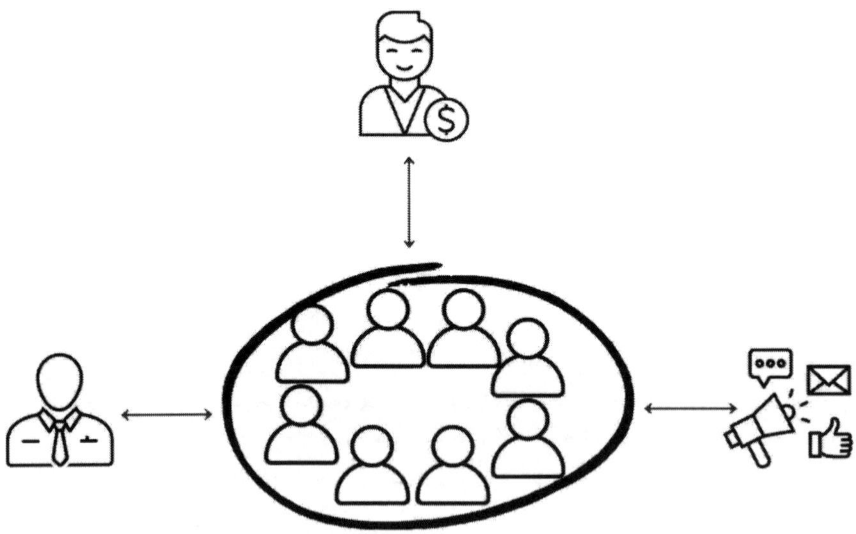

There are no managers in the cell, yet the members are self-operating. Cells set goals for (personal) growth, performance, and well-being. As they do not have any salespeople internal to the cell, revenue should be weighed less heavily compared to performance, growth, and, for instance, how many assignments get closed due to cell members getting hired specifically by name. Goals could look like this:

Dedicated:	Topic:	External to cell, but connected:
- 9+ average evaluations by clients - Achievement of goals toward vision - Each month, x number of content posts - Number of new vs deprecated courses - X number of active teaching days	- 9+ average evaluations by clients - Achievement of goals toward vision - Consultants 85% of time billable - Active teaching days - Latest trends in topic highlighted in the portfolio	- X number of revenue (differs per type of cell) - 9+ cell member happiness ratings - Fair, individual compensation

The image below depicts an organization with multiple service lines (Digital Journey, Microsoft Services, etc.) and different areas of operation (consulting, training, etc.). Within these service lines, there are multiple cells—both dedicated and topic cells. The Digital Journey Service Line (SL) has multiple cells. This might be because individual trainer cells are focused on a specific topic, so there would be a focused training cell around a specific topic (Agile Leadership, Product Academy). There are no existing cells around Partnerships and Off-the-shelf-Solutions, meaning they are handled differently. This takes us back to the first chapter of this book—to think about what makes the most sense for your situation. Not every part of the organization benefits from Scrum; equally, not everyone benefits from working with cells. Also, this is a simplified version. The bigger the number of people involved, the higher the number of cells would be advised for communication reasons.

All the above elements should align with the organizational vision and strategy to achieve desired outcomes.

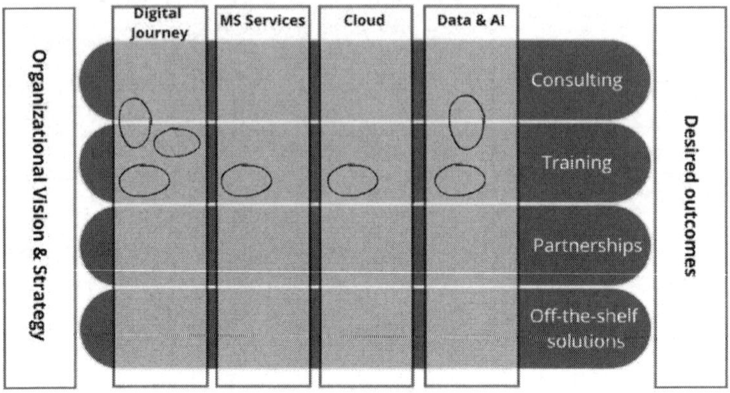

Figure 48 - Each oval represents a cell.

There are many ways of scaling. There are plenty of scaling frameworks. Some are truly beneficial; some have a buzzing, cash-grabbing marketing machine. We won't go into the specifics of which are which because we want to stay on the safe side (or do we really?). Each has pros and cons, like any framework. But before closing this chapter, we want to repeat ourselves once again in a final attempt to make it stick: Nail. It. Before. You. Scale. It.

Ryan and Sander's Summary Feed (RSS Feed)

If there are any points that we want you to take away from this chapter, they are as follows:

- Start by ensuring the foundation is done right before doing anything related to scaling up.
- When there might be more work than the product team can handle, challenge them to think of possible solutions. This supports self-management.
- Adding more people adds more complexity as communication lines grow. Adding more people to an already late project will delay it further than speed up delivery.
- Before scaling up, consider scaling down first. What can we *not* do in our backlog, or how are we organized to maximize the output?
- If the need still exists to scale up, do it organically. Create new teams around the most experienced people and hire new people for the original team. This will mean a temporary dip in performance, as new people need to get accustomed to the new environment.
- Adding a scaling framework to an existing organization without making any changes will not deliver any results, either. Change accordingly, cutting the waste out of the system and product.

Reflection

Use this page to reflect on the initial questions at the beginning of this chapter and what you may have uncovered throughout.

What do you notice in your organization in scaled efforts?

If you were to lead the scaling effort in your organization, what would be the first thing you would do?

How do you coordinate work across multiple teams?

10.

Leadership for Value

"It is not the strongest of the species that survive, nor the most intelligent, but the one most responsive to change."

– Charles Darwin

Preflective Questions

Management and leadership are concepts that are mixed and misunderstood by many. The fact that one is a manager does not make him a leader. We would argue that mixing these two is more harmful than helpful, sometimes even destructive to the general workplace atmosphere. Rarely do we get managers in our classrooms to be at the forefront of change, yet in their environments, they are in Leadership Teams and consider themselves leading the change. How can one lead something they don't understand? Leading the organization into the ground, sure. But not in the desired direction. From now on, we disconnect these two concepts (imagine us whipping our wands and *poof*, disconnected) even when you re-read this book (which we hope you will) so that you don't rely on managers to lead the way.

Who leads the change initiatives in your organization?

How do you know if changes are working?

Are you a leader, a follower, or an anchor of legacy?

Flash backward a year ago, just after Roy's meeting with the board and the decision to start applying Scrum. Sabrina has been feeling anxious lately. She has a strong track record of getting things done and understands project management to its core. That has been her entire career. Besides the lack of understanding of the new way of working, she can't help but think about how it could endanger her obtaining the yearly bonus that's based on the product she's responsible for. If this change in delivering other products does better than she can, she risks not getting the bonus she often already spends before it hits her bank account.

She reads the Scrum Guide and researches this framework, which seems disruptive to her job. Worried she will lose her job, she figures it's better to keep a close loop with Roy and the rest of the team so she can still be involved in the day-to-day operations. Feeling a solid bit of FOMO (Fear Of Missing Out) for not coming up with the whole Scrum idea herself, she decides this might be the next best option. She discusses her concerns with John, too, using slightly different wording.

"Do you really think these people are going to save our company? They know nothing about the product or our culture. Why don't we do this the way we know and have always done things? That's how we got big in the first place. Remember how I led our first-ever major success story? The only thing that needs to change is that our developers need to work harder and better. And probably longer, too, because I highly doubt they're working the amount of hours they claim."

John shares her concerns and doesn't make it any better by saying she's probably correct. "I see your point. I constantly wonder what I'm paying these people for. However, we're in a tough spot, and that didn't happen without reason. It's incredibly hard to keep up with the pace of the competition. These projects are just too cumbersome before they deliver any value. And truthfully, I constantly want to jump in and take over whatever Roy is doing. He should have done things a lot differently and been stricter with his team. Ruling with an iron fist has always been my approach during my days as a project manager."

Sabrina frowns, frustration evident in her voice. "Can't we just offer them a bag of money? Work more hours, get more money? I've seen companies have their developers work weekends. Why don't we do that?"

John sighs and shakes his head. "And where are we supposed to get that money from? We're already low on cash, let alone spending more for more hours. I highly doubt the quality of our work would go up."

"Well, what if I could prove Roy wrong? That Scrum isn't the salvation he thinks it is. What if I make the exact same product except doing it my way? I'm confident it will be delivered faster and with better quality, too!" The passion in her voice is impossible to miss. Sabrina begins formulating a plan to go behind Roy's back. It would involve many late nights, but she has a loyal group of colleagues ready to support her in creating a solid plan to outcompete her internal competitor.

Sabrina has been developing biometric security machines for long-standing government clients, so she knows exactly what to build. To ensure she doesn't miss any options, she consults her former clients, who trust her. Adding their input to the requirements list, she now has an extensive list of everything that needs to be built. One challenge she faces is having no idea how her development is compared to Roy's team.

Maybe I should use their own framework against them by joining their Sprint Reviews, she thought, immediately sending Roy a message to invite her.

At the end of the third Sprint, six weeks into development, she receives quite the opposite of what she had hoped for. The first Sprint Review, where some high-level clients participate, show Roy and his team demonstrating a working prototype of a fingerprint scanner. It already has basic encryption, a simple user interface, and, most importantly, a smooth ergonomic design that is aesthetically superior to any similar device the company has ever made before. The client is overjoyed with what has been developed in such a short timeframe, exceeding their expectations. However, there are still concerns.

Manuel, Chief of Security at Pineappolis International Airport, is cautious. "Let's not get carried away here. This is the first time we're seeing anything working—impressively, I might add—but it's just a prototype. I appreciate what you've created, but what's to say other companies won't be able to do the same thing? I've heard that the new big airport in Dubai will get the fanciest technology money can buy."

Roy responds with calm assurance, "And I'm sure these companies are very aware of that. They understand their client can buy anything they want, and that comes with a price. We're being totally transparent here. You see exactly what you get, how much we've spent on it, and it's up to you to decide whether you want to keep investing." This was his opening to strengthen the relationship.

Sabrina feels a swirl of emotions. On one hand, the team's success—one she was quietly trying to outperform—leaves her feeling a mix of envy and relief. The company's survival means job security, after all. Yet, uncertainty gnaws at her. She seizes Roy's open invitation to Manuel to voice her concerns.

"All this so-called transparency is great," she began, "but it doesn't show any long-term commitment. Shouldn't we assure our customers we know what we're doing? It's not our first time building these machines. We need a roadmap with deliverables so Manuel can plan accordingly."

Roy, Jax, and the rest of the team sit in stunned silence, blindsided by the internal politicking. This isn't the transparency they were hoping for.

"Maybe we need to discuss this internally and come up with a plan," Peter says, visibly annoyed by what he sees as a lack of respect. Sabrina takes the non-committal response as a sign that the team is clueless, a smirk tugging at her lips. The monthly steering committee meeting follows the Sprint Review, with both Roy and Sabrina in attendance. The tension is palpable.

"All right, you two, what's going on?" Karen demands, looking between them. "You've been sniping at each other and undermining each other's initiatives. Do you not realize we need both of you to succeed? The company isn't in the best shape, and this infighting is making it worse."

Caught off guard, they stay silent for a moment. "I just don't get why we need this new methodology!" Sabrina bursts out.

Roy, already briefed by Jax, mutters, "It's a framework," under his breath.

"Tomato, potato," she shoots back dismissively.

"No, it's not the same," Roy retorts. "And that's why this mess is happening. You don't understand the change. We're all trying to save this company. As you saw earlier, we're finally on the right path to compete. Now you want to undermine that?"

Jax is called in as a voice of reason to provide some clarity on Sabrina's role in the new setup.

"You see, management and leadership are not the same. In this complex world, we need *leaders* with management skills. We can't predict the future, but we need effective managers. John has been micromanaging our developers so much that Ronda moves her stuff whenever he walks by to avoid his scrutiny.

We get your fear and uncertainty, but this can't continue. To be blunt, John needs to steer the company's direction, and we need you, Sabrina, to create an environment where our developers, Roy, and I can ensure top-quality products. We *need you*. But we have to figure out how to do that together, without the political games."

Where do we go from here?

Starting something new requires courage. You'll need to find the trailblazers,[31] the ones with the guts to do what hasn't been done before. The rebels who don't stick to the ways they already know so well, who are comfortable being uncomfortable. This is true for both team members and stakeholders. Suppose we're working with risk-averse stakeholders who don't feel comfortable investing in experimentation and the creative freedom in problem-solving by the product team. In that case, we'll likely spend more time putting out the fires between our stakeholders and the rest of the team. It takes proverbial cojones to get started and form a path in the corporate jungle for others to walk on.

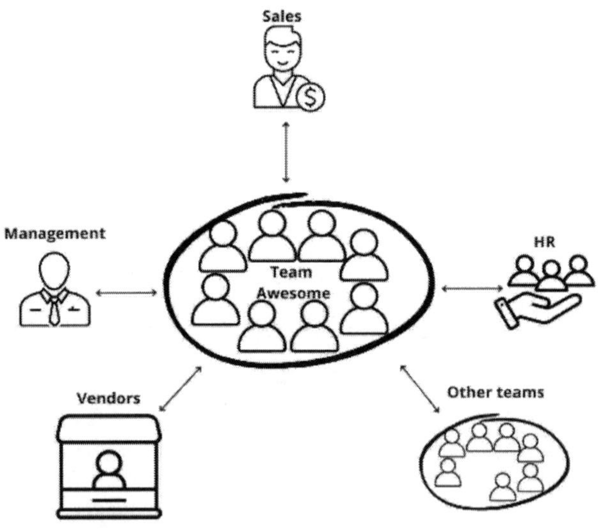

Figure 49 - Change is not only for the product team.

The newfound leaders will need to collaborate with other parts of the organizations that are not working in the same awesome way. Awesome—doesn't that sound a bit unprofessional? Maybe, but if we as team members don't feel

[31] *https://www.scrum.org/resources/blog/why-you-should-be-looking-organizational-trailblazers*

this new way of working is awesome and inspiring, why should we even start in the first place?

When we gain traction, we spread the knowledge and experience to other domains and teach what we have learned.

Leading the Foundation

The foundation doesn't get built by itself, and it cannot be built alone. Organizations need true leaders to create pathways, show better ways of doing business, or create products. As there are no best practices in modern complex domains, there is no blueprint we can apply for others to follow. Start by finding like-minded people to generate momentum.

Build Champions for Change

Find someone in an executive position responsible for a product's success that could not be created without a new development method. These champions, especially when high in command, can support the product teams and create an environment shielding them from disruption and undesired distractions.

The opposite is equally destructive as champions are constructive: when we focus on the naysayers, it will take exponentially more time and energy to get the change in motion, if in motion at all.[32]

Be Wary of the Pollution Trap

Many product teams act as if resources are limitless and abundantly available for them to deplete. We're definitely not saying that this is done consciously or deliberately, but it is equally easy to get carried away in the realm of opportunity and vision. *"If only we could have two more months," "We're almost there; we just need to..."* If we don't pay attention to acting correctly and focus on doing what is most valuable right now rather than six months from now, soon we'll be feeding the marshmallow monster again, and our ideas will end up on the Graveyard Backlog.

These constraints can be both physical and virtual. If we purchase more inventory than we need, we'll soon need more storage space. If we create a massive product that requires tons of maintenance on features, we won't even measure it

[32] *Kotter, John, "Our Iceberg is Metling"*

anymore, so much tech debt will creep in that it will be impossible to keep a stable product.

My own personal Pollution Trap at the beginning of my career was the future version of me I had in mind. I always saw these Portfolio Managers around me with a lot of perceived status, big fat BMWs, and high salaries. Unconsciously, I was more focused on getting into that position than doing my current job well. This resulted in poor performance in the job I was supposed to do. I filled my mental backlog with all kinds of things that shouldn't have been there. This led to me burning out. Apparently, status, money, and BMWs are not great motivators. Who knew?

Funding Like a Startup

Many teams we've worked with were granted a budget for the entire year, if not longer. This is good in some aspects, but it also has downsides: it's much easier to become complacent when there is sufficient budget. We can lean back and slowly do our job, right? Well, lean is the good word, but not leaning back.

Startups have to budget carefully, as funds are limited. They rely on the success of their initial product's advancements before hopefully making it big. The majority of products never make it big. According to Investopedia[33] the most common mistakes by startup leaders are:

- Not budgeting;
- Burning cash too quickly;
- Not doing their research;
- Lack of target market;
- Failing to establish a business plan;
- Hiring employees too quickly (i.e., scale too quickly).

Let's treat our new endeavor like a startup, even when we're working for a massive incumbent. Define a high-level vision, a Product Goal to have achieved at least by the end of those three months, and some experiments to get there. At the end of those three months, we can validate whether we, together with the stakeholders (read: investors), deem the results worthy enough for another round

[33] *https://www.investopedia.com/articles/personal-finance/040915/how-many-startups-fail-and-why.asp*

of investments. This way, we'll foster a mentality of doing that which is absolutely needed to achieve this goal.

Sandbox

Many of us developed social and fine motor skills, improved our hand-eye coordination, and lived in a world of imagination and creativity in a magic place called the sandbox. Again, it is one of those places where the realm of possibilities exists. And at some point, without knowing it, you left that sandbox for the last time. And in many cases, that's also where a part of imagination and creativity is stranded. As time progresses, we are being taught, drilled if you will, to think inside boxes rather than outside. When we now need to be creative in our adult lives, it becomes hard to do so.

What if we told you we want you to get your hands dirty in the workplace? We want you to probe, sense, and respond. That might sound scary, we know! Trust us, we sometimes still feel uncomfortable being the corporate equivalent of a toddler. Yet, that is where many ideas are born. Not all of them are equally valuable, but they are a great way of figuring out what ideas might be valuable. And the funny thing is that it is contagious to many of you who feel they can be human again rather than suited zombies. Sandboxes encourage engagement with others and, by doing so, increase the diversity of perspectives and ideas.

If you are leading your organization or team, we want to challenge you to create a sandbox for others to discover. Help them become or remain creative but also develop boundaries. Like physical sandboxes, there is a limit to where it is safe to experiment and play. These boundaries provide guidance and direction.

Strategize for Value

Inspired by the work of Dave Snowden's *Process of Strategy,*[34] we mapped our experience and interpreted it in these process points. Sandboxes are great, but we cannot stay in them forever. Roaming freely, ideas can decline product value or even damage others when no (ethical) boundaries have been set.[35]

---

[34] *Dave Snowden, Process of Strategy https://thecynefin.co/the-process-of-strategy-3-of-3*

[35]*https://www.forbes.com/sites/zacharyfolk/2024/01/23/pharma-bro-martin-shkreli-still-banned-for-life-from-pharmaceutical-industry/*

As a leader, you are responsible for helping people see the impact of their behavior, whether positive or negative, and for assisting others to "mature" in the process.

Constraints and Boundaries

AI is a great example of a current jungle scene, maybe even a Wild West scene. It is one of the biggest modern hypes; everyone wants a piece of the pie. This is leading to almost uncontrolled growth and application of AI tools. This wild growth needs boundaries, too, before things spiral out of control. In December 2023, European Union lawmakers achieved a political agreement on a draft AI act to create a framework around the use and supply of AI systems in the EU.[36]

The purpose of these boundaries is to create consistency, protection, and guidance for participating members to follow. This prevents different member states from doing something differently, potentially harming others. Examples are data protection in line with GDPR, data processing rules in the public interest, and sandbox standardization between local and European guidelines. These boundaries create cohesion as well. To put this into an organizational perspective, the lack of these boundaries can lead to multiple departments battling each other for the king of the hill, seemingly forgetting that they work for the same organization. Inevitably, we're creating multiple guerrilla organizations operating under the same flag. This misalignment is displayed and becomes cluttered and a waste for the organization to disband. Also called reorganizations, which no one likes, yet easily preventable by clear constraints and boundaries. A very small example of a boundary is the Definition of Done. A broad example is the degree to which AI developers can go wild with collected data.

Measure

After establishing and practicing our constraints, we need to measure which ones work and which don't. For the ones that do not work as intended, we need to identify to what extent we can change them to make them work for us rather than against us. How much time and energy are required to change them? Is it a sensible investment to change them? What scenarios hinder these factors?

Let's take the DoD as an example. Typically, the more experienced and mature product teams become, the more stringent the DoD becomes. If we make these

[36] *European Union, 2023, Artificial intelligence act and regulatory sandboxes*

quality checks rigid and abundant for a team still discovering the lay of the land, they'll be more consumed by the nitty-gritty of the product—as if they are counting the grains of sand over building a castle. Creativity gets stifled, and we put our product team back in the box. The one that we wanted to free them from in the first place.

Amplify or Dampen

The ones we found helpful can be either left alone or amplified, fed to grow to become even more supportive, and the soil for the team to thrive. The ones that are not helpful or even damaging to creativity, growth, or productivity need to be dampened to acceptable levels, destroyed until they are entirely removed, or distracted so that they do not get in the way of success.

Hypothesize

Identify or create hypotheses that could cause positive change while also setting boundaries to these hypotheses. When do we know whether we are right? How much time can pass before we continue or abandon this hypothesis? Who should be involved?

Strategizer cards, as discussed in a previous chapter, can be input for these hypotheses, as could Cynefin's concepts.[37] A hypothesis we've seen organizations experiment with is building teams to full agency. These hypotheses take time, sometimes even years, but they are fully beneficial for the success of the involved product teams.

Convey

Explain the intent throughout all levels of the organization. Intent does not mean goals. Goals are specific and measurable objectives that structure our actions (think about how Sprint Goals are steppingstones toward Product Goals), whereas intent is the underlying motivation and purpose. Intent is essential for success within the organization and brings us back to the start of this book: understanding the why behind our endeavor.

This often has the side effect of more people wanting to join the product team and your leadership—it is contagious, and people want to be part of the

[37] *https://thecynefin.co/*

awesomeness. Still, be wary of rapid expansion—restrict scaling even though getting caught up in momentum and enthusiasm is easy.

Lead by Example

Few things are more impactful than leaders eating their proverbial dog food (please do not eat dog food). Showing humility, humanity, and confidence in the taken direction builds trust. People will want to follow without being forced to do so. It feeds the sense of purpose but mostly autonomy and agency that they *can* be part of change but don't *have* to. We don't expect you to know everything—we expect you to be honest. If you're unsure about the path forward, say so. People will poke holes in imaginary confidence quickly and bail on participation. Authenticity is vital in leadership. The opposite is true, too; if you tell people to go left while you go right, they'll be confused and start questioning your intent. Planting little seeds of doubt quickly diminishes results and feeds mutiny.

Figure 50 - Leaders need skin in the game to lead the journey.

We've all seen these so-called leaders. They pretend to have the best interests of others at heart while their double agenda is to ensure their bonus over the backs of others. Be transparent, foster trustworthiness, and be the leader you want others to become. Leadership is not about being in front of yourself but guiding others to greatness, regardless of our personal agendas. Seeing people in your leadership sphere shine is a leader's most significant achievement.

Fading Upon Necessity

Creating leaders has additional benefits for you, too. You can start fading when they rise, but support them when they need it the most, creating a perpetual loop. When we have led others to self-sufficiency, we can discover new areas or products or enjoy the success we've created with our current product. But like every other product, this success will stop at some point; we must always keep moving. This is why continuous experimentation is essential for corporate sustenance. Without experimentation, we'll be left in a rut of complacency.

The dictionary defines complacency as "a feeling of self-satisfaction, especially when accompanied by a lack of awareness of actual pending trouble, deficiencies or controversy."

"But hold on. Didn't you say something about a lacking burning platform and "we've always done it this way?""

Yes, we did! Corporate complacency is a real thing, unfortunately. It leads to self-satisfaction levels so high that people become so confident, almost arrogant, about their work that it creates a downward spiral. Arrogance leads to shortcuts. Shortcuts create technical debt. Technical debt leads to poor quality, which leads to micromanagement. Micromanagement leads to the Eye of Sauron watching all. In this case, there is no relationship between fading upon necessity and the Eye of Sauron.

We, as leaders, need to prevent corporate complacency and foster self-vigilance. A state where people and teams become open about positive impacts and situations, where they can share feedback and concerns, ultimately becoming alert of opportunities to develop and capitalize on product value and team strength. This enforces the self-sustenance of leadership on all levels.

Leadership Antipatterns

Even when leaders mean well, they still make mistakes sometimes. It's almost as if they are human. Unaddressed mistakes often become antipatterns, becoming the managers they want to avoid becoming. We could write an entire book about this, but for now, we chose to summarize them here.

Overcompensation of insecurities: Everyone has insecurities—some more than others—and that is okay. Overcompensating those insecurities, on the other hand, is not. This often leads to an unbalanced relationship in the workspace, with one person dominating situations or lashing out. If you feel insecure about something, address it. Seek help if necessary. But do not make others the victims.

We need to know everything: *"What, that's an antipattern? Knowledge is power, right?"* To a certain degree, sure. However, it's unrealistic and even harmful to expect yourself or someone else to know every detail about the product, the process, people's personal lives, etc. There's only so much you can store in your memory. It's a recipe for disaster if anything. Knowing whom to contact for certain expertise gets you further healthily.

Atlas alias: We think we have to bear all responsibilities alone. There's a reason it's called teamwork and organization. The whole team is responsible for the product's success, and the entire organization is responsible for creating an environment for growth. You do not have superpowers, nor do you need to.

Figure 51 - You don't have to carry the world by yourself.

Top-down works best: *"The people at the top of the food chain are there for a reason; they have experienced everything! They have graduated at the best Ivy League universities!"* Cool, well done to them. The world does change after graduation, though. People closest to performing the work should be empowered to decide what's best given the circumstances. Whether that's work at the top or the bottom in the (hypothetical) hierarchy.

Leaders learn last: We often see the (self-) perceived leaders as the last to be educated. Again, you're not leading, you're lagging. Get your butt into a classroom asap. How can you expect results from others your lead if you don't even know the dynamics of the framework yourself?

Utilization maximization: We think busy people are the ultimate measurement of progress, but this is untrue. Their hands may be moving, but the output is stagnant. They're so busy being busy, finishing work is almost a bad sign. Because now they have extra capacity, that's not good! Focus on optimizing the flow of work and output. Henrik Kniberg has a great, short clip about this.[38]

Overly policing: *"I didn't see you online on MS Teams today until 9:02; you were supposed to start at 9:00." "The Daily Scrum took seventeen minutes, not fifteen!" "Your shirt is on backward; that's against policy."* Seriously, no one likes that. Okay, maybe in the latter case, it might be useful to turn your shirt correctly. But no one benefits from constantly over-policing every single little letter of the rulebook. When it's a pattern and detrimental to value delivery or the overall atmosphere, yes, step in, but don't keep people under a microscope.

Calling people resources: It's disrespectful. A laptop, the keyboard we wrote this book with, and Olina's (the graphic artist for this book, thank you very much) Neuland markers are resources. You can pick them up and throw them around; no harm done. But don't put people in the same category. If we catch you doing so, you'll have to sing a song in public.

Trust, but verify: If you feel the urge to verify, you can't trust. It's as simple as that. Is there a reason to distrust others? Then, address it and improve.

I need to change them (other people): No, you do not. They are good as they are (some extreme exceptions excluded). You can't change someone else. You can only lead by example and hope others will follow. This is the way.

Leading is challenging and sometimes even scary. It can be very rewarding when all goes right but equally thankless when things don't go as expected. Leaders need feedback, too. Don't be afraid to ask others around you about your leadership.

[38] *https://youtu.be/CostXs2p6r0?si=3BWvpHBGqhj4NHed*

Ryan and Sander's Summary Feed (RSS Feed)

If there are any points that we want you to take away from this chapter, they are as follows:

- Leadership is *essential* for success and does not mean management.
- Focus on the people who favor change to generate momentum. People who are reluctant to change require more energy and are more likely to put a brake on change.
- Enthusiasm is great, but it can also bring more ideas than required—leading to waste in the product or organization. Keep things as lean as possible.
- Helping others be creative and use their mental capacity requires a bounded sandbox in which to experiment. Spoon-feeding things to do only creates zombies.
- Ideas and activities supportive of change should be amplified or left alone, while those that hinder change should be destroyed or dampened.
- Include the broader organization in the results of the new path. Share the results and try to create more champions.
- You can't change others; you can only display desired behavior for others to follow or mirror.
- You don't have to do everything by yourself as a leader. You cannot carry all the responsibilities on your own.
- Leadership requires perseverance to stick.

Reflection

Use this page to reflect on the initial questions at the beginning of this chapter and what you may have uncovered throughout.

Who would you consider to be leaders in your organization?

Who should be leaders but are not leading?

How would you describe leadership to someone else?

FINAL WORD

Product Management and Development are incredibly challenging. Although we refer to Scrum throughout this book, it is not the only framework for delivering value to stakeholders. As the team at Magnum Opus demonstrates, it is easy to do things incorrectly, as it can be confusing to make decisions in a complex world. While they made many mistakes, at least they are trying to improve, which is more than we can say for many organizations.

Everything you've read here, all of the stories and anecdotes, happened in our consulting gigs. We've changed the names of the people, but the scenarios are real. We don't know about you, but we constantly find it hard to identify what works and what doesn't in the vast ocean of books, tools, models, theories, and LinkedIn Influencers out there. The most important thing we've learned that doesn't work is copying what everyone else is doing. What does work, is having a good, hard look at your (work) environment and making assumptions about what *could* work. Try that, learn, and improve. Amplify or dampen. There is no blueprint for success. And gladly so, we must say. Else, we would be out of jobs.

Magnum Opus, particularly Roy, embodied the lack of response; leaning on legacy success does not guarantee future survival. We've seen (and continue to see) many organizations live the same story without realizing it. Sticking to the by-now-common metaphor of children, these organizations are like infants; they want to run so eagerly that they get frustrated and need to learn how to crawl first. But there's no short-cutting evolution, only poorly executed imitations with myriad dysfunctions and antipatterns. Many of which you've read about in this book.

The crux for us is in the word *evolution*. Commonly referred to as "the Agile Transformation," the imitation mentioned above starts. Because a transformation implies that we go from state A to state B or back, like a Transformer. In the world of Transformers, these transformations are the Decepticons. There is no end-state in agility. We constantly have to inspect and adapt, probe and respond. Try, fail, learn, repeat. This makes it a journey, a constant evolution, because it does not end, unlike a transformation.

Let the lessons in the Magnum Opus universe inspire you to achieve greatness. If there is a sequence of steps (we would recommend accepting the lack of a blueprint), it would be this:

- Hypothesize;
- Apply;
- Validate or reject;
- Learn and ingrain;
- Start again from the top.

Yes, we realize it does not give you any clarity on how to run your product management. We're a little afraid that if we were to give you more details and steps, we would become like the non-existent Spotify model. That started with Henrik Kniberg's video on the Spotify Engineer Culture published on YouTube, which was perceived as the latest, greatest model for others to copy.

Ultimately, it doesn't matter what framework, method, or process you choose. Whatever it is, apply it correctly and stick to it for a while. Only then will you know whether it works or not. We can guarantee it *will not* work if you cherry-pick whatever elements you like (like running your Daily Scrum once a week. Seriously?).

Involve your stakeholders and sit down with your users, but don't assume value. Keep the feedback loop short to capitalize on opportunities and mitigate risk. Before you know it, you'll see the product's value grow. Involve other departments, vendors, and your competitors' products. Apply the sequence mentioned before and have the courage to kill your ideas equally. Value doesn't only come from "doing the things right," but just as much from "doing the right things."

Throughout writing this book, we've relived the frustration we experienced in our consultancy. Sometimes, it's hard to maintain sanity in a world where everything may seem so evident to you but completely different to others. Trust the change process, lead by example, and keep going if you believe something is right. If you can validate that you're right, that would be even better. Find your champions, generate traction, and then expand it. As our good friend Ravi Sandhu would say, *"Land and expand; don't spray and pray."* Reflect on your progress toward goals and assess whether or not to continue.

If you are still with us reading this, thank you so much for your curiosity and perseverance! We admire you and would love to hear your thoughts. By all means, connect with us. It has been an incredible journey for us to put our thoughts into this format, and even though Ryan's dedication said he's not doing this again, The story isn't over for Magnum Opus...yet.

Sander and Ryan, out. *mic drop*

Acknowledgments

Behind the authors of every book stands a community of people who helped refine the ideas, improve their expression, or create time to read the concepts conveyed in the material. This book is no exception and would not exist without the support and encouragement of many people.

Our colleagues in the Scrum.org community, whose commitment to better products and ways to build them, continue to challenge and inspire us; Dave West and Maarten Dalmijn to carve out the time to read and foreword this book; Robbin Schuurman and Willem Vermaak to challenge our models and ideas; Jim Sammons to always be the echo chamber in our conversations.

Our graphic designers, Olina and Sabrina, whose work made this book and the Magnum Opus story come to life. Without these graphics, the humanity (and stupidity) of our characters would have been hidden behind our writing. We are glad that Olina and Sabrina had the patience to work with us.

Our amazing Discord community, where we could empirically improve this book by running A/B tests with ideas, writing snippets, and initial drafts; in particular, Marge Scheuerer for always making time to review our latest versions and graphics; and Gillian Holle-Sammons for sharing insights and experience into your personal challenges in the product management realm.

Our many clients, colleagues, and trainees, over the many years of our careers, have shaped our views on product management and whose experiences inspired us to create Magnum Opus and the storyline of this book. We are grateful for the pain, arguments, and successes that we've shared with you all. Life and work can be pretty boring unless you have wonderful people to share it with, so thank you.

To our group of friends called de Bezems, particularly Robert, Wesley, and Mark, for starring in our Persona formats.

Our loving families, who patiently supported us and gave us the time to write, rewrite, and contemplate the purpose of life after the millionth iteration, ultimately publishing *Solving for Value.* When starting out, we both agreed that writing a book was some small way of existing forever. Well, we are now immortal.

Our final acknowledgment is to you, our dear reader. Thank you for picking up and reading this book. We are incredibly honored that you chose this one out of the ocean of others, and we truly appreciate it.

About the Authors

Sander Dur

Sander Dur is a Professional Scrum Trainer at Scrum.org, Professional Trainer and Lead Agile Consultant at *Xebia*, founder and podcast host at Mastering Agility, and public speaker. He gained experience as a Scrum Master, Agile Coach, and Leadership Consultant in many top-tier organizations, including Nike, GrandVision Latin America, Sky Media, and ASML.

As a recovered Project Management Officer, Sander found his new life energy in Scrum and business agility. This is evident from the classes he has taught internationally, the articles he has written on various related topics, and his podcast, Mastering Agility.

Connect with Sander:

https://www.linkedin.com/in/sanderdur/
www.masteringagility.org
https://www.scrum.org/sander-dur

Ryan Brook

Ryan Brook is the Director of Training at Optilearn and a Professional Scrum Trainer at Scrum.org. He primarily works within large public and private organizations in the UK, supporting leadership and teams to improve value delivery. His previous clients include BAE Systems and Lockheed Martin.

He is an ex-teacher who previously worked as a Head of Subject in a UK secondary school before transitioning into the world of Professional Scrum. As such, he holds Qualified Teacher Status and uses these skills in his training classes. He also enjoys speaking at international conferences and supporting the wider Scrum community.

Connect with Ryan:

https://www.linkedin.com/in/ryan-brook-pst/
www.optilearn.co.uk
https://www.scrum.org/ryan-brook

About Xebia

Xebia explores and creates new frontiers. Always one step ahead of what businesses need, we turn the latest technology trends into advantages for our customers. As a mainstream frontrunner, we create new solutions and build the future with our clients. An international network of passionate technologists and pioneering craftsmen, Xebia provides cutting-edge tools, training, and consulting services that make businesses work better, smarter, and faster.

Founded in 2001, Xebia was the first Dutch organization to embrace the Agile way of working with gurus like Jeff Sutherland. Since then, we have grown from a Java company into a full-service digital consulting company with 5,000 professionals working on a worldwide ambition.

We are organized in complementary chapters—teams with tremendous knowledge and experience in a particular field, such as Agile, DevOps, Data and AI, Cloud, Software Technology, Security, Low Code, and Microsoft Solutions.

We help the world's top 250 companies and category leaders overcome digital challenges, embrace innovation, adopt new technology, and implement new business models. In addition to high-quality consulting, we also provide offshoring and nearshoring services.

Contact:

https://xebia.com/

Address:

Laapersveld 27

1213 VB Hilversum, the Netherlands
+31 (0) 35 538 1921

About Optilearn

Founded to support individual learners

Optilearn is primarily a training organization founded to support individual learners' professional development.

We don't plan to do things the same way as other large corporate training providers, mainly because that's not what we want to be.

We are proud to work with Scrum.org as part of their Training Network. This means that our classes are accredited and validated for their quality. In turn, this gives you confidence that any class you take with us will be delivered by the very best trainers.

Contact:
Gloucester, UK
enquiries@optilearn.co.uk

https://optilearn.co.uk/contact/

About Mastering Agility

Mastering Agility started as a podcast series hosted by Sander Dur and Jim Sammons that aims to inspire listeners to drive value, improve the way they work, and how they can adapt to complex environments.

Topics discussed vary widely, depending on the guest speaker(s). This podcast will discuss anything related to product management and business agility, whether it's people, frameworks, technical challenges, user experience reports, or anything else. But since the start of the podcast, we've evolved.

Rapidly becoming the largest community-wide content platform, we serve not just podcasts anymore. Currently, there is a Discord Community, Medium publication, meetups, merchandise, and much more planned for the near future.

Website:

https://masteringagility.org

Discord:

https://discord.gg/masteringagility

Medium Publication:

https://medium.com/mastering-agility

Meetups and events:

https://www.meetup.com/nlscrum/

Printed in Poland
by Amazon Fulfillment
Poland Sp. z o.o., Wrocław

44058801R00145